DODGER'S
LONDON

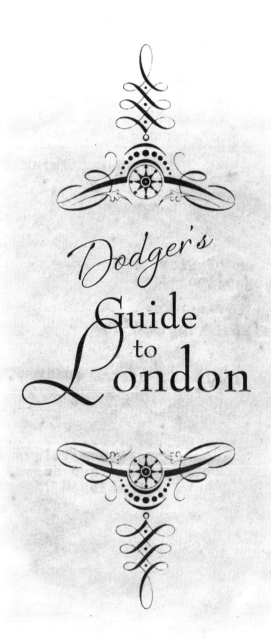

Dodger's
Guide to London

·❦ Also available ❦·

Movements and Marvels: A Guide to the Underground Sewage System
by Col. H. Fawcett

———✴———

Fun in the Gutters: Games and Pastimes for Poor Children
by Mrs Emily Button

———✴———

Employment Opportunities for the Under Fives
by the Rev Amos Smallpiece, Chairman Whitechapel Poor Relief Fund

———✴———

A Turd in the Hand: A Tosher's Life Recalled
by 'Daffy' George

———✴———

Long Drops for Little Necks: Cautionary Tales for Children
by Mr Jeremiah Bloat, Former Chief Hangman at Rochester Gaol

———✴———

A Rough Guide to the Rookeries
by 'A Bene Cove'

———✴———

Rising Damp: Living Conditions in Seven Dials
by Lady Eudora Bloombe

———✴———

Up a Chimney with a Dead Goose: Recollections of a Retired Chimney Sweep
by Mr Thaddeus Plant

Terry Pratchett

PRESENTS

Dodger's

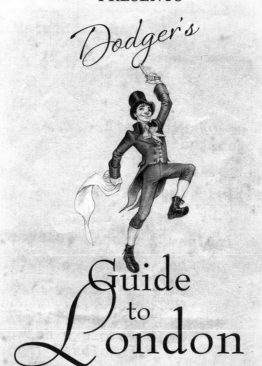

Guide to London

(with an especial interest in its underbelly . . .)
Based on original notes penned by
Jack Dodger himself

DOUBLEDAY

DOUBLEDAY

UK | USA | Canada | Ireland | Australia
India | New Zealand | South Africa

Doubleday is part of the Penguin Random House group of companies
whose addresses can be found at global.penguinrandomhouse.com.

www.penguin.co.uk www.puffin.co.uk www.ladybird.co.uk

Penguin
Random House
UK

First published 2013

003

Text copyright © Terry and Lyn Pratchett, 2013
Illustrations copyright © Paul Kidby, 2012, 2013
Considered trifles courtesy of The Discworld Emporium, Wincanton, Somerset
Text design by Lizzy Laczynska
Picture research by Liane Payne

The right of Terry Pratchett to be identified as the author of this work has been asserted
in accordance with the Copyright, Designs and Patents Act 1988.

Set in 10/13 Minion Pro

Printed in Great Britain by Clays Ltd, Elcograf S.p.A.

A CIP catalogue record for this book is available from the British Library

COLLECTOR'S EDITION ISBN: 978-0-857-53324-1

All correspondence to:
Doubleday, Penguin Random House Children's
One Embassy Gardens, 8 Viaduct Gardens, London SW11 7BW

MIX
Paper from
responsible sources
FSC
www.fsc.org   FSC® C018179

Penguin Random House is committed to a
sustainable future for our business, our readers
and our planet. This book is made from Forest
Stewardship Council® certified paper.

For further copyright information see page 138.
Every effort has been made by the publishers to contact the copyright holders of the material
published in this book; any omissions will be rectified at the earliest opportunity.

·❧ CONTENTS ❧·

──·❦ Introduction ❦·──

Way back in the late 1840s – in the time of Victoria and Albert – a young nobody by the name of Dodger (a name he gained solely due to his ability to dodge trouble) – rose from the sewers to become a hero of London. His notes on the London he knew so well – from the poorest streets, where his ability to urch made him an urchin of the highest calibre, to the top corridors of power, where he was able to hob (if not hobnob) with the nobbiest of all – became the inspiration for this guide.

Mister Henry Mayhew's monumental work – *London Labour and the London Poor* – gives the reader an amazing amount of factual detail about life at this time; but for those who, like Twain or Disraeli, believe that there are 'lies, damned lies and statistics', then Dodger's colourful notes bring Dickensian London to life more easily – showing as they do everything from the honey wagons on their nightly patrols around the streets to collect the golden harvest* to the seedier areas of the London Docks, where unwitting visitors would be swiftly divested of all they bore and all they wore – in some cases, even their lives, with an unplanned, bracing swim in the river in the middle of the night.

I have taken the liberty of updating the notes for the modern reader, also adding a few timely additional points appreciated from the vantage point of compiling this little book 150 years after Mister Dodger's original observations.

Terry Pratchett,
Salisbury, UK
2013

*Piss.

About Sir Jack Dodger*

Born into poverty, raised in an orphanage, young Dodger was a tosher, a scavenger in the sewers, proving time and time again that where there's muck, there's . . . well, at least some occasional silver. Through his brave deeds and exploits – in particular in helping to capture the infamous Mister Sweeney Todd – Dodger rose to prominence, being knighted by the Queen for services to his country. As 'the right kind of scallywag' to work for the government, he then had the time of his life breaking laws all over the world (apparently it's not breaking the law if done on the orders of those who make the laws), and being paid handsomely for it.

*Dodger, of course, is a fictional character, and some of Dodger's associates – like Solomon, Miss Simplicity and even Mister Sweeney Todd – are also fictional; but the world they inhabited most definitely was *not*. Victorian London, in all its glory – and filth – follows, presented as though seen through the eyes of a young Dodger of the time.

·❦ A Note from Jack Dodger ❦·

When I was a kid, I thought I knew every dirty inch of London – where it was safe to go, and where not. I knew everybody who was nobody, and the square mile was my whole world. Especially the tunnels beneath the streets, where I spent many a happy hour splashing through the muck.

London is where I comes from, and a body never easily forgets the streets he or she grows up in. They are what has helped to make me the man I am today – a man who is happy as both a gentleman and a tosher (though truth to tell, sometimes there is very little difference betwixt the two).

And so, for your entertainment, I have taken the liberty of penning a few notes about London. But this might be a London that is new to you. For I gives you a portrait not just of a glittering metropolis, but also one of the street folk, and orphans and little matchgirls, with rascals of the first order on every corner. A city where a geezer needs to have eyes not just in the back of his head, but probably in the back of his arse too.

I trust that you will find my little booklet most entertaining and instructive. And should you dare in the future to venture into the rookeries alone, you will likely return without leaving behind your pocketbook and/or your boots.

Jack Dodger

Jack Dodger,
London
1872

SPECIE AND SLANG

In which, before we move on to Dodger's London itself, we provide a small visitor's guide to some of the essentials, without which life could become very confusing indeed.

·❧ Specie ❧·

The universal currency. For the tosher grubbing around in the muck, a silver crown was a good week's work – though he might not have called it a crown, but a *bull*. Visitors to London were often bemused by some of the local terms used for the currency of the time. Here are some details of the coinage of the era:

£1 = 1 sovereign = 20 silver shillings (20s)

1 guinea = £1 1s

1 shilling = 12 pennies (12d), making 240d to the pound
   (1 shilling was also known as a *bob,* or a *hog*)

5 shillings = a crown, also called a *bull*

2s 6d = half a crown, also called a *half-bull*

6d (six pence) = also called a *tanner*, or a *sprat*

1 farthing = 1/4 of a penny

'As for sprats, we always say they are God's blessing for the poor' – coster girl to Mister Henry Mayhew, *London Labour and the London Poor*

'Annual income twenty pounds, annual expenditure nineteen [pounds] nineteen [shillings] and six [pence], result happiness. Annual income twenty pounds, annual expenditure twenty pounds ought and six, result misery' – Mister Micawber, in the novel *David Copperfield* by Charles Dickens (1850)

Take a Butcher's at My New Crabshells!

And here are some of the more colourful terms you might have heard
on the streets of Dodger's London:

Barker: a gun

Beak: the magistrate

Blag: to steal or snatch, often by smash-and-grab

Blows up: scolds

Bluebottle: a policeman

Boat, get the (*boated*): to be sentenced to be transported to another country, or just to get a very harsh sentence from the beak

Brass: money

Bruiser: a boxer

Buck cabbie: a dishonest cab driver

Butcher's, take a: take a look (rhyming slang from *butcher's hook*)

Buzzing: stealing, pickpocketing

Candle to the devil, to hold a: to be evil

Cant: a present

Chink: money

Chiv, shiv: a knife, razor or sharpened stick

Choker: a clergyman, or a neckcloth

Clink: a prison

Cocker: a pal, friend

Coopered: worn out, no use

Costers: those working in the greengrocery trade, selling fruit and veg off stalls or carts

Cove: a man

Crab, to: to snitch on someone

Crabshells: shoes

Crib: where someone lives

Dipper: a pickpocket

Dollymop: a prostitute, often just part-time or a girl in service making some naughty money on the side

Fence: someone who sells stolen goods

Flam: a lie

Flash-house: a relatively safe meeting place for criminals, with beer and naughty ladies – often used by fences

Flimflammer: a cheater, someone who deceives or cons you

Fluefaker: a chimney sweep

Flying the blue pigeon: stealing roof lead

Growler: a four-wheeled cab

Half inch: to steal (*pinch*)

Hammered for life: married

Holywater sprinkler: a club spiked with nails

Jerryshop: pawnbrokers

Judy: a woman, with the term often used to mean a prostitute

Lobcock: a willy

London particular: a thick London 'peasouper' fog

Lump Hotel: the workhouse

Moniker: a signature or name

Mot: a woman, especially someone running a lodging or public house

Nibbed: arrested

Nipper: a child

Nobble: to inflict grievous bodily harm

Nose: an informer or spy

On the fly: moving quickly

Peeler: a policeman

Penny gaff: a cheap theatre

Piccadilly weepers: a type of gentleman's whiskers

Raws: your bare fists

Rookery: a slum or ghetto

Screever: a forger, a dodgy lawyer

Snakesman: a slim lad used to break into houses

Snuff, up to: sensible, a cove you could do business with

Specie: money

Spouts: speaks

Stumps up: pays

Tea leaf: a thief

Ticker: a watch

Titfer: a hat (*tit for tat*)

Toff: a stylishly dressed gentleman

Toolers: pickpockets

Topping: a hanging

Trotter cases: boots

Whistle: a suit (*whistle and flute*)

THE CREAM OF THE CAPITAL

Now let's begin at the top with a bestiary (because they think they are the best) of the nobbiest nobs in all of London. I was fortunate to once meet the royal couple and I thought Queen Victoria was a splendid-looking girl – though very nobby, of course. And Prince Albert had that . . . special handshake that Solomon seemed to recognize. – Jack Dodger

❧ Queen Victoria and Prince Albert ❧

The top couple in . . . well, most of the world at that time, since the British Empire covered so many territories, the mapmakers probably ran out of red crayons to colour the maps.

DID YOU KNOW?

- ❀ Victoria was only 18 years old when she became queen in 1837. She was wearing just her dressing gown when the Archbishop of Canterbury and Lord Conyngham told her the news. She went on to rule for almost 64 years. This was longer than any other British king or queen and the longest of any female ruler in known history.

- ❀ Her childhood nickname was 'Drina' – a shortening of her full christened name of Alexandrina Victoria.

- ❀ She was only 5ft (1.52 metres) tall.

She married her German cousin, Albert, in 1837. They had nine children, 40 grandchildren and 37 great-grandchildren – although the queen hated being pregnant and thought newborn children were ugly.

 Victoria found the idea of breastfeeding so repulsive that when her daughter, Alice, chose to breastfeed her own child, she purportedly named a dairy cow after her.

 Between 1840 and 1882, there were seven attempts to assassinate Victoria.

 She was crowned Empress of India in 1876.

"NEW CROWNS FOR OLD ONES!"
(ALADDIN *adapted.*)

Coronation gaffes

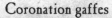 At the Coronation, Lord Rolle, who was 82, fell and (with his name, you couldn't make it up!) *rolled* down the steps when coming to do homage to the new queen.

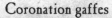 The Archbishop of Canterbury put the ring on her wrong finger.

A little black dress?

After her husband died (aged only 42), Victoria always wore black. Most Victorian widows wore black for two years, and then went into 'half-mourning' – they could wear both black *and* as many shades of grey as they liked. Victoria wore black for *forty years*!

10.50 p.m.

That's the time at which Albert died in 1861 – and all the clocks in his room were halted then. But Victoria didn't just stop there. She wanted Albert's valet to pretend the prince was still alive, so he had to carry on taking soap, towels and hot water to Albert's room every day, even laying out clothes for him to wear.

A Prince Albert

Sadly, for all his many accomplishments, Prince Albert has become most known for his championing of a piercing and ring on a very personal part of his anatomy, making him the first prince reputed to wear jewellery in his nether regions.

·❧ The Great Exhibition ❧·

A huge supporter of both industry and the arts, one of Albert's achievements was the wonderful Great Exhibition of 1851, also known as the Crystal Palace Exhibition. Thousands of exhibits were on display, ranging from the world's biggest known diamond (at the time) to the 'Tempest Prognosticator', a barometer that used leeches.

DID YOU KNOW?

Building the Crystal Palace took just 35 weeks; St Paul's Cathedral had taken 35 years!

Cross your legs . . . a queue of 827,000 people for the jakes!

When going to the loo usually meant a second chance to look at yesterday's dinner, a toilet which amounted to more than a hole in a bit of wood over a bucket was a wondrous thing. And even more wondrous was . . . a loo that flushed! Only the nobbiest nobs in London had one of those, but at the Great Exhibition up to 11,000 ordinary people *a day* got to use the jakes and then pull a chain with a little porcelain knob on the end of it.

It was surely waiting to be pulled, wasn't it? But why? To let people know that you had finished? Did it ring a bell so that people didn't come in and disturb you?

──·❧ Buckingham Palace ❧·──

The palace was built on a piece of land that was planned by James I (1603–25) to be a mulberry garden – where he could rear silkworms. Sadly for the toffs who wanted silks for their unmentionables, James chose the wrong kind of mulberry bush and the project failed . . . (though apparently the bushes were put to good use, as the gardens later became known as a place of debauchery).

DID YOU KNOW?

 Queen Victoria was the first monarch to live at Buckingham Palace. But as Dodger and other urchins gazed in wonder at the magnificent building, they didn't know that the chimneys smoked so much that it was often freezing cold inside.

 The palace now has 775 rooms, including 19 state rooms, 52 royal and guest bedrooms, 188 staff bedrooms, 92 offices – and 78 bathrooms.

In-I-go Jones

An apothecary's errand boy named Jones was found sneaking into the palace in 1841 on more than one occasion – not to harm Her Majesty, but just to hide under a sofa near her bedchamber.* In a witty comment, Lady Sandwich stated that the little scamp must undoubtedly be a descendant of the architect In-I-go Jones.

Dodger supposed he'd have made a good snakesman . . .

---

* Although according to one source, he once got caught by the police with a handful of Queen Victoria's unmentionables stuffed down his trousers . . .

—————·❧ Lady Angela Burdett-Coutts (1814–1906) ❧·—————

More specie than almost anyone else in the world – and she gave lots of it away!

Heiress when still very young to her grandfather's fortune of around three million pounds,* Lady Angela Burdett-Coutts was a most unusual woman, and a very powerful one in an era when women did not yet have the vote. Most amazingly, *she gave lots and lots of her money away.* She had lots, of course – but it's still pretty astonishing.

DID YOU KNOW?

 Lady Angela was a big supporter of the 'ragged schools', which aimed to help children get a bit of an education – and hence a bit of a chance of poking their heads up from the foggy streets of the rookeries (where the fog was so thick and black at times you could not only taste it but take a knife and fork to it, then extract the soot and make a fire).

 A true friend to animals and wildlife, Lady Angela was President of the British Beekeepers' Association, the first patron of the British Goat Society, set up drinking fountains for dogs and was closely involved with the RSPCA.

 She famously once proposed marriage to the Duke of Wellington, who turned her down – the Iron Duke could face Napoleon, but Lady Angela was a battle he reckoned he wouldn't ever win.

 She finally got married at the age of 67 – to her 29-year-old secretary.

---

* That's a huge sum of money, roughly £130,000,000 today. A lot of specie in anyone's book!

·❧ The Ragged Schools ❧·

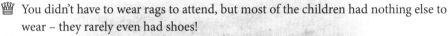

'Can read 'beer', 'gin' and 'ale'. No sense in filling your head with stuff you don't need, that's what I always say.

♕ You didn't have to wear rags to attend, but most of the children had nothing else to wear – they rarely even had shoes!

♕ Charlie Dickens provided a water trough for a school, 'so the boys may wash'.

♕ School classrooms could be anywhere – in old stables, lofts or railway arches.

♕ Classes focused on the three 'R's – *reading*, *'riting* and *'rithmetic* – with a whole load of Bible study thrown in so the children could name the apostles even if they couldn't find anything to eat (unlike Dodger, who famously couldn't name an apostle to Charlie Dickens, but was *very* skilled at getting hold of a dinner).

A good fire along with a bit of learning

In *London Labour and the London Poor*, a young mudlark of the time explained how he was attracted to the school by other boys: 'They told me that all the boys used to be laughing and making game of the master. They said they used to put out the gas and chuck the slates all about. They told me, too, that there was a good fire there, so I went to have a warm.'

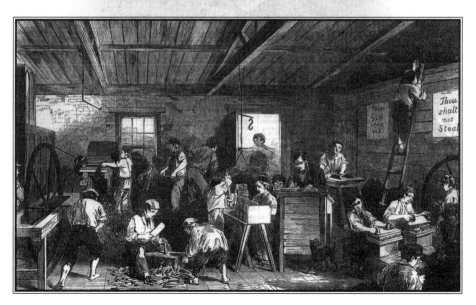

·❧ Benjamin Disraeli (1804–81) ❧·

A definite geezer.

DID YOU KNOW?

- Disraeli was Britain's first, and so far only, Jewish Prime Minister (first term in 1868; second from 1874–80).
- A smooth-tongued Conservative politician, he described his success as having 'climbed to the top of the greasy pole'.
- Gladstone – his political rival – reputedly once told Disraeli: 'Sir, you will probably die by the hangman's noose or a vile disease,' to which Disraeli is rumoured to have replied: 'Sir, that depends whether I embrace your principles or your mistress.'

The Wisdom of Solomon: 'If I was you I shouldn't think too much more about politics, it can only make you ill.'

One nation – that needs two bottles of brandy?

In a landmark speech in 1872, Disraeli spoke of the country being divided twixt the rich and the poor; he coined the term 'one nation' for his hope for the future. It was a long speech – and apparently Disraeli consumed two bottles of fine brandy whilst giving it! So he was undoubtedly rather worse for wear by the time he had finished his talk about helping the poor . . .

Westminster and the Houses of Parliament

This place was just another rookery: bigger, warmer, certainly richer, definitely better fed to judge by the stomachs and the redness of the noses, but just another street where people jostled for advantage and power and a better life for themselves if not for everybody else.

DID YOU KNOW?

The Houses of Parliament are considered a royal palace, so it is illegal to die there. Anyone who does so, however, is entitled to a state funeral.

Remember, remember ... er, the 16th of October

Guy Fawkes couldn't manage it (though as Dodger once heard a cove claim, 'No man ever went to Parliament with better intent'), but when a couple of workmen spent nearly 11 hours throwing wooden tally sticks into a furnace in 1834 . . . they managed to burn down both the House of Commons and the House of Lords!

A filthy habit

Smoking was banned in the House of Commons in the 17th century – presumably so that no one could burn the place down – but snuff was provided as an alternative. Even today, there is a full snuffbox by the door of the Commons.

When the tongue is mightier than the sword

Politicians fight their battles in debates. But just in case anyone gets any ideas, the two red lines on the floor of the House of Commons are apparently just over two sword-lengths apart.

The Wisdom of Solomon: 'The lords and elected members debate the issues of the day in Parliament itself, but I strongly suspect that here in London the actual outcomes have a lot to do with the things that people say to other people over a drink.'

ASPIDISTRA LAND

In which I introduce you to the middle classes – marooned out in the suburbs – oh, as far out as Chelsea, where the smells of the river coil and loop their way round your head and into the pores of your skin and every crease of your unmentionables, but mean that houses are affordable to the up-and-coming. So, that's all right, then.

Feeling themselves far superior to the common working man, and aiming to look like gentry, the middle classes used their homes as one way to demonstrate their status – and a pot plant, something like an aspidistra, often took pride of place in the front window. The overall impression might be of affluence, but Dodger and his snakesmen friends knew that the houses were often just all show – like a lady of the night whose painted face and velvet cloak promised heavenly delight, but whose body had gone so far south it had revolved around at least one pole more times than you could count on one hand.

Too nobby to cook and clean

Although many of the middle classes lived life on tight budgets, one expenditure was vital: about £10 a year for a servant. No respectable middle-class Victorian would have felt their household was acceptable in society without at least one person to clean up after them – to dust all those oh-so-essential little ornaments.

Dodger was a great one for noticing little ornaments, especially the kind that could be picked up very easily and shoved into a pocket at speed and sold again almost as fast. But what was the point of them? To show that you could afford them? How much better did that make you feel? How much happier were you really?

·❦ Mister Henry Mayhew (1812–87) ❦·

Friend to Charlie Dickens, Mayhew recognized that the poor of London needed more than the occasional soup kitchen. He made it his life's aim to research the conditions of life for those in the grubby underbelly of the richest and most powerful city in the world.

DID YOU KNOW?

 Henry knew about large families – he was one of 17 children himself.

He ran away from Westminster School after he refused to be flogged by the headmaster, Dr Goodenough. Good enough for whom? we wonder.

He was the editor of the first editions of *Punch*, and thereafter a 'suggestor in chief' for them.

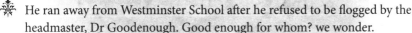

·❦ London Labour and the London Poor ❦·

Mayhew walked the streets of London chatting to everyone he met: to young girls selling bunches of violets or sharp-tongued coster lads on their barrows. He provided a hugely impressive document filled with facts and statistics that showed in astonishing detail the reality of life amongst London's poorest.

👑 *London Labour and the London Poor* began as a series of articles for the *Morning Chronicle* in the 1840s, and was then published serially until Mayhew had a row with the printer over money. It was later published as three volumes in 1851 with a fourth in 1861.

👑 Each volume had about 500 pages – printed in double columns!

I've seen wives working alongside their husbands on the street stalls, and young girls working their fingers to the bone to save their families from starving, so although man is the master – all right and proper, of course – I've got a lot of respect for the ladies, too. And nobody can tell one of them girls working the coal barges what to do, f'rinstance – some of them have fists on 'em as big as coal shovels themselves.

'No man, I am told, can be a slave. I trust, gentlemen, that this applies to ladies as well' – *Miss Simplicity*

But sadly Simplicity was only partly right. Although there was a woman on the throne, a man was in charge of nearly every other woman in the land. For a Victorian female wasn't legally a person at all – just a piece of *property*, belonging to her father and then her husband. And any wife would be sent back to her husband if she tried to run away, even if she had good reason to do so.

If a man wanted a divorce, he only had to prove his wife had been having a bit of hanky-panky with someone else. If his wife wanted the marriage to end, however, she had to prove that her husband hadn't just been hankying, or pankying, but doing the whole caboodle, probably also involving close relatives or a small furry pet.

Unmentionables

If nobby women were considered weak and hysterical, blame their unmentionables. By the 1840s, a woman in the best possible circles could easily be dragging herself into the dining room wearing as much as 40 pounds of clothing, including:

- a dress and hoopskirt (crinolines were made using whalebone or steel to create a hoop that would give shape – but the voluminous skirts could easily catch fire and the wearer would be burned to a crisp)
- a knee-length chemise
- a camisole
- half a dozen petticoats
- a corset
- drawers.

Now try and eat a decent pie!

DID YOU KNOW?

- The crinoline could be truly fatal – there were tales of women being swept off piers by gusts of wind and carried out to sea, where they drowned (who could swim with a steel cage round your waist?).
- Tight-laced corsets could also be deadly. Breathing the wrong way when wearing one could actually break a rib!

Victorian beauty secrets

First published in 1873, *Beauty: What It Is, and How to Retain It* set out some very useful tips:

- 'At night the teeth should be cleaned with a very soft brush of badger's hair.'
- 'The water used for washing the skin should be rain-water, but if London rain-water, it must be filtered to clear it from smuts.'
- 'Hair should be brushed for twenty minutes night and morning.'

The battle between the sexes, according to *Punch* magazine . . .

In his corner:

HINTS TO MAKE HOME HAPPY
TO HUSBANDS

• KEEP UP THE PRACTICE of reading the paper during the whole of breakfast time; of allowing yourself to be spoken to half-a-dozen times before you answer, and then of asking your wife what it was that she said. Upon her telling you, make some reply which is nothing to the purpose, as if you were thinking of something else.

• VERY OFTEN ORDER DINNER punctually at five, and very seldom come home till a quarter to six. Occasionally, however, return at the appointed hour, and, not finding things ready, complain that you are never attended to.

• [. . .] IN SHORT, on all occasions, consult studiously your own inclinations, and indulge, without the least restriction, your every whim and caprice; but never regard your wife's feelings at all; still less make the slightest allowance for any weakness or peculiarity of her character; and your home will assuredly be as happy as you deserve that it should be.

PUNCH (Jan.–Jun. 1844)

And in hers:

HUSBAND-TAMING.

But to each according to his birth! And here I offer you a few small notes on the teeming mass of humanity making an honest – or dishonest, if necessary – living. For if the workhouse doesn't beckon, it is necessary for most to find some occupation that brings in a bob or two. The London I grew up in is filled with people using what they have in order to get by in life, with the lucky ones – depending on the trade in question, of course – getting to work with their dad and follow in his footsteps, even if them footsteps are only one step up from the gutter. So take it from me, the old baked-potato-selling lark is all the go, very reliable; why, I sees one bloke doing the baking with his wife and kids dishing them out to the mob. He was a clever cove, he was, and paid to use a baker's oven when it wasn't needed and was selling those potatoes hand over fist. Always a good risk, your potato. Keeps people on the streets warm all night, especially the crusty ones. Potatoes, that is, because most of the people on the streets was crusty themselves.

Mister Solomon Cohen told Dodger how he once met a rather hairy young man (Mister Karl Marx) with new Ideas about Workers and Downtreading and Capital and Masses – but the average working man wanted none of that. A day's pay for a day's work was fine – even if that particular day's pay was barely enough to feed one man and keep him in beer. Downtrodden? No, though certainly trodden on – by horses, donkeys, those Worse for the Drink, or even the occasional pig.

Had Dodger not been a tosher by trade and a gentleman by luck, he might have expressed an interest in joining these other venerable professionals.

·❧ Knocker-uppers ❧·

When a body wasn't sure what work he'd be doing the next day – labour could be offered on a daily basis – he needed to employ the services of a knocker-upper to wake him up. For 6 pence a week, the man would hammer on your door and make sure you rose from your slumber. The poor knocker-upper himself might need to wake someone at 3 a.m. in one part of the city, then get himself over to another district by 3.30 – and in all weathers, making about 9 shillings a week. He'd often gain a free hair wash in the process, as neighbours of the man to be woken expressed their discontent by chucking the contents of water pails (or worse) over the poor knocker-upper's head.

——·❧ Dockers ❧·——

The hub of the Empire was built on the backs of the dockers, and any notes on London must surely include reference to the famous dockyards – a forest of masts with flags from all nations fluttering amidst the smoky skies. Huge sheds – some four storeys high – were stacked to the gunnels with baccy, pungent hides and horns, spices and goods from all over the Empire. Shops and stalls lined the quays, eager to part a jolly Jack from his specie. And dodging and bobbing amongst the crowds were the London wharf rats – children eager to do anything that might earn a penny to stave off hunger.

DID YOU KNOW?

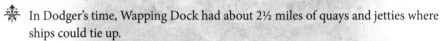

❋ Up until the end of the 18th century, Wapping waterfront was the site of Execution Dock – a scaffold where pirates and mutineers were hanged. Pirates were often hanged with a shortened rope so that they died slowly, and their bodies were then left on the dock until three tides had washed over them.

❋ In Dodger's time, Wapping Dock had about 2½ miles of quays and jetties where ships could tie up.

❋ Sometimes there could be as many as 300 ships in the dock, and the warehouses were filled with more than 200,000 tons of goods.

❋ One of the warehouses was just for tobacco – storing up to 24,000 hogsheads of baccy! (A hogshead is about 1,200 lb, so that meant about 30,000 tons.)

❋ One of the wine vaults had an area of seven acres – and all the wine vaults together could stow 60,000 pipes of wine (a pipe was approx. 475 litres).

So London folks clearly liked their wine and baccy, and perhaps something else as well . . .

By the time I was twelve I knew the words that meant 'Where are the naughty ladies to be found?' in lots of languages, including Chinese and several African ones. Every wharf rat knew those; and the naughty ladies might give you a farthing for setting a gentleman's footsteps in the right direction.

[Note: As Dodger grew older he realized that some people would say that was, in fact, the wrong direction.]

——— ❧ Navy Jacks ❧ ———

The naughty ladies didn't just hang around the docks with their eyes on the sailors from the merchant ships – Navy jacks were also perfect customers, coming on shore with their pockets full of pay and just ripe for a bit of slap 'n' tickle in one of the 'houses of ill-repute'.

JACK ASHORE.

Policeman. "HOLLO, JACK! I SUPPOSE YOU'RE NOT SORRY TO COME ON LAND FOR A BIT?"

Jack (who hasn't got his shore legs yet). "WELL, IT AIN'T SUCH A BAD PLACE FOR A DAY OR TWO—ONLY IT'S SO PRECIOUS DIFFICULT TO WALK STRAIGHT."

Homeward Bound – an old fo'c'sle song that pretty much sums it up

'It's now three years that we've been out,
I think it's time we tacked about,
And when old England's shores we see,
Oh won't we have a jolly, jolly, spree,
For we are homeward bo-o-ound,
For we are homeward bound.

'And when we get to the London Docks,
There we shall see the girls in flocks,
One to another they will say,
"Welcome Jack with his three years' pay,"
For he is homeward bound.

'And then we go to the Lamb and Bell,
Where very good liquor they do sell;
In comes the landlord with a smile,
Saying "Sit down, Jack, it's worth your while,"
For you are homeward bound.

'But when your money is all spent,
And there's nothing to be borrowed, and
nothing to be lent,
In comes the landlord with a frown,
Saying "Get up, Jack, let John sit down,"
For you are outward bound.

'And so poor Jack, without a crown,
And scarce a place to sit him down,
Is quite cleared out of all his store,
So goes to sea to work for more,
For he is outward bound.'

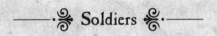

——— ·❀ Soldiers ❀· ———

A shilling to sign, a penny thereafter . . .

Recruiting was often done in a public house where a lad – often with beer in his guts and dreams of glory in his head – would accept the queen's shilling (especially if he was unwise enough to accept a drink in a tankard without a glass bottom). After that, pay was about 1 shilling a day, but 'stoppages' meant that many got less. In 1847, it was made law that a soldier had to get at least 1 penny a day.

DID YOU KNOW?

 Most military medals were made from the gunmetal of Chinese cannons.

Troops serving abroad could still be flogged right up until 1881. In the Napoleonic Wars (1803–15), a soldier could be sentenced to up to 1,200 lashes – enough to kill him! Back in the time of the Peninsular War (1808–14), one soldier was sentenced to 700 lashes for stealing a beehive.

THE GREAT MILITARY-CLOTHING ESTABLISHMENT AT PIMLICO

In that dreary part of Pimlico which abuts upon the river Thames, close to Messrs. Cubitt's great building establishment, the government have lately dropped a little acorn, which, in time to come, will, without doubt, develop, as government acorns so well know how to do, into a gigantic oak. We allude to the new Military-Clothing Establishment which seems to have sprung up here in a night.

[. . .] There are 380,000 boots and shoes, of all sizes, built into the brown-looking bastion, that first greeted our eyes in this Brobdingnagian establishment, and these were not all. At regular intervals, all down this long room rose what we may perhaps be allowed to call haycocks of boots – Wellingtons for the cavalry, so disposed with their feet in the centre, and their long upper-leathers hung outward, as to form huge cones of leather.

'But,' said we to the commissariat-officer who obligingly conducted us round the establishment, 'how are soldiers fitted?'

'Oh,' he replied, 'we make half a dozen sizes, and they are sure some of them to fit.'

– Extract from *Pictures of Town & Country Life, and other papers* by Andrew Wynter (1865)

One boot only . . .

The wars with the French (under the Froggy general, old Boney) left behind many victims – old sweats thrown back on the streets, sometimes with only one useful foot, the other a wooden leg; sometimes taking to crime with a knife in their hand – as Dodger discovered when he ran into Stumpy Higgins trying to rob the *Morning Chronicle*. What use was a medal if you only had one leg?

I know now that there are many types of war, and many types of hero.

·❧ Skilled Craftsmen ❧· ——

While a dock labourer just needed strong arms and a tough back, and a thief needed a quick hand and an even quicker set of heels, it took a lot of practice before a man could make a decent (or *indecent*, if required) pair of boots.

Dodger's good friend, Mister Solomon Cohen, was renowned for his skills in mending jewellery, clocks and other precious objects. He cleaned, shaped, bent . . . and made the world a better place in his own small way.

Solomon was never *hard* at work – he was always soft at work, almost always on tiny things that needed tiny tools and considerable amounts of patience.

DID YOU KNOW?

 A craftsman's wage was usually about double that of a labourer.

Skilled craftsmen like bricklayers, masons and carpenters were paid 6s 6d for a ten-hour day when building the first section of the Victoria Embankment in the 1860s.

'In coorse God Almighty made the world, and the poor bricklayers' labourers built the houses afterwards' – sixteen-year-old coster lad to Mister Henry Mayhew, *London Labour and the London Poor*

And a less honest trade . . . ?

Dodger's own skills, however, had a slightly less honest purpose. He put his talent into customizing those little friends who might gain him entry to a crib, especially those cribs that were sewn up tighter than a duck's arse (which everyone knew was watertight – no bad thing if any duck was unwise enough to swim in the waters of the Thames). He spent many a happy hour with his rakes and picks, bending and filing them into exactly the right shapes, getting them ready to go into battle.

Popping a weasel?

When work was scarce, even the skilled craftsman often resorted to pawning his tools at the pawnshop – you couldn't eat a hammer or a saw, after all. Dating back to the 1700s, an old children's rhyme uses Cockney rhyming slang about 'popping' (pawning) a 'weasel' (a weasel and stoat, meaning coat) when the money in the house ran out . . .

'Half a pound of tuppenny rice,
Half a pound of treacle.
That's the way the money goes,
Pop! goes the weasel.
Up and down the City road,
In and out the Eagle,
That's the way the money goes,
Pop! goes the weasel.'

Though it also suggests that the money might have run out by being spent in the pub – the Eagle was an old public house in Hackney, rebuilt as a music hall in 1825.

——·❧ Fluefakers – Chimney Sweeps ❧·——

The soot, it gets in everywhere, everywhere. Into every cut and scrape, and it's perilous stuff; does very nasty things to your unmentionables . . .

Up the chimneys of our great metropolis

Being a skinny lad – ideal for climbing up one of London's myriad sooty chimneys – Dodger himself was once apprenticed to a sweep, but he didn't take to the life – or more particular, he didn't take to the soot.

DID YOU KNOW?

❧ Some of the climbing-boys only washed once in every six months.

❧ The average sweep claimed that beer was essential to wash away the soot that lodged in his throat.

❧ If Victorians couldn't afford to pay a sweep, they might drop a goose down their chimney instead to clean it.

'They spend their time and what money they may have in tossing for beer, till they are either drunk or penniless. Such men present the appearance of having just come out of a chimney. There seems never to have been any attempt made by them to wash the soot off their faces. I am informed that there is scarcely one of them who has a second shirt or any change of clothes . . .'
– Henry Mayhew, *London Labour and the London Poor*

SWEPT
FLUES CLEANED
I OFFER A MOST SUPERIOR SERVICE.
CLEAN, RELIABLE
AND UNSURPASSED IN DILIGENCE TO YOUR WISHES.
MY ASSISTANTS ARE KEEN, NIMBLE & CAPABLE OF ENTERING THE SMALLEST FLUE OR CHIMNEY.
PRICES FROM 3d to 6d
ALBERT PLANT
12 CLACK St, WAPPING.
CHIMNEYS

————·❦ Servants ❦·————

An army of nobodies, working for the somebodies

The front of a crib was for the nobs who lived there, but the back was for the servants – cook, kitchen maid, maid-of-all-work, scullery maid and anyone else prepared to spend their lives on their knees polishing floors so that somebody upstairs didn't have to.

An urchin at the door

A piece of pie or mutton could easily be forthcoming if the household cook had a soft spot for the poor little lad who was such a cheerful young chappie . . . and Dodger himself could out-urch most of the other urchins with one hand tied behind his back (and the other hunting for some little knick-knack that was looking for a new home). Of course, although the cheeky chappie was the chap who got the pie, many urchins had problems with being cheeky, given that it was hard to have good plump cheeks when you were living on pennies.

Advice to the household about what they can expect from their domestics . . .

'The routine duties of cook, kitchen-maid, and scullion being intermingled, can scarcely admit of separate descriptions. The cook directs the whole business of the kitchen; the others assist in its performance; she is responsible for the mode in which it is conducted and performed, and must possess, therefore, adequate skill; they, on their part, have only to be active, cleanly, and obedient. To these domestics, early rising is of the utmost importance . . . not later than 6 in the summer and 7 in the winter.'

– Extract from *An Encyclopaedia of Domestic Economy* by Thomas Webster (1845)

Advice to the domestic servants about what they should expect . . .

PUNCH'S GUIDE TO SERVANTS

————————

'"First catch your fish" is a golden rule for a cook, and *first catch your situation* is a very necessary piece of advice to be given to servants in general. The choice of a mistress requires as much judgment as the choice of poultry; and you should be careful not to pick out a very old bird in either case.

THE MAID-OF-ALL-WORK
Do not be too inquisitive at first, for you will have other opportunities for a good rummage.'

– PUNCH (Jul.–Dec. 1845)

A NATION OF SHOPKEEPERS

Solomon once told me as how the Froggy general Napoleon described the British as a 'nation of shopkeepers'. * *I don't know about that – in the rookeries, it is more like a nation of chancers – but it is true to say that there are shops about for anything a body might wish to buy, as long as he had specie in his pocket.*

Victorian London contained a large army of shopkeepers, clerks and other aspiring middle-class workers, who had pulled themselves up by their boot-straps and had absolutely no intention of letting go. And if a young lad were to be possessed of a rudimentary education (as opposed to the rude stuff he'd learned on the streets) and wore a shonky suit on his back, he might be able to enquire as to a position in one of the city's many retail outlets – he might even aspire to a lowly role within one of London's massive emporiums in the nobby districts. And for those with the jingle of silver in their pockets, the shops and retail establishments of the metropolis fully justified their high reputation worldwide.

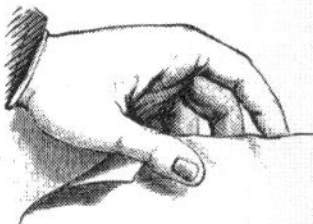

DID YOU KNOW?

- Lock & Co. of St James's Street made the first bowler hats, after being asked to design something for a Norfolk gentleman's gamekeepers. They were called 'coke' hats after the gentleman in question, a Mister Coke.
- The first Sainsbury's store was opened in London in 1869 by John James Sainsbury and his wife Mary Ann.
- Harrods store introduced the first 'moving staircase' in 1898 – and a glass of brandy was offered at the top to help calm nervous customers.
- Burlington Arcade – a covered walkway near Picadilly Circus with 72 shops in it – was opened in 1819 to sell jewellery and 'fancy articles of fashionable demand'. To protect customers from undesirables (pretty much everyone Dodger once knew would have come into this category) it was patrolled by beadles wearing top hats and frockcoats.

*He didn't come up with this witticism on his own, since it was borrowed from a cove called Adam Smith in his book *The Wealth of Nations*, published nearly a hundred years earlier.

Dodger himself first experienced the joys of attending such an establishment as a welcome visitor (rather than going in through the fanlight as a very *unwelcome* visitor) when Solomon took him to Lock & Co. to buy a hat fit for a gentleman. Any young man aspiring to look like a gentleman would look much closer to being a swell when wearing an elegant hat (even if the body below *did* still smell rather less salubrious).

And buying a hat was a serious business for any gentleman . . .

NATURALLY THE FEMALE THINKS SHOPPING VERY FOOLISH AND TIRESOME.

Superior Creature. "FOR GOODNESS' SAKE, EDWARD, DO COME AWAY! WHEN YOU ONCE GET INTO A SHOP, THERE'S NO GETTING YOU OUT AGAIN!"

For those with less specie, the smaller stores in areas such as Whitechapel – pawnbrokers and shonky shops, butchers and barbers – beckoned. Dirt, dust, thieves and rats were an optional extra. And if a London butcher ever gave away a bone for a dog, it was a given that it wasn't just near the knuckle, but the knuckle had already been boiled for soup and what was left had given up any idea of providing anything one might usually expect to find on or in a bone.

·❧ Buy! Buy! Buy! Street Sellers by the Score ❧·

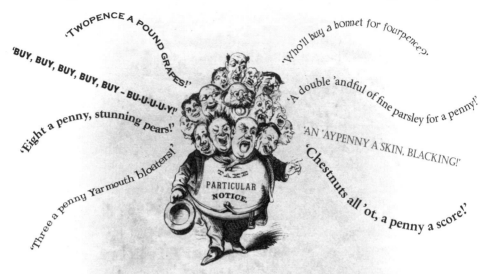

'TWOPENCE A POUND GRAPES!'

'Who'll buy a bonnet for fourpence?'

'BUY, BUY, BUY, BUY, BUY - BU-U-U-U-Y!'

'A double 'andful of fine parsley for a penny!'

'Eight a penny, stunning pears!'

'AN 'AYPENNY A SKIN, BLACKING!'

'Three a penny Yarmouth bloaters!'

'Chestnuts all 'ot, a penny a score!'

TAKE PARTICULAR NOTICE.

A candlestick made out of a turnip

All of London would be out buying, nicking or selling at the markets – especially Saturday nights, when the light dwindled and the lamps were lit: red, smoky flames from grease-lamps, the startling white from a new gas-lamp, or just a candle stuck in a bundle of firewood or a turnip. And the markets were full of bounty – low-hanging fruit and other delights that a young lad could 'rescue' from falling onto the ground as it somehow fell into his own mouth.

> Among the market stalls Solomon could haggle even a Cockney until the man gave in – and Heaven help any stallholder who sold Solomon short weight, bad bread or rotting apples, let alone a boiled orange and all the other tricks of the trade, including the wax banana.

You could buy … fish, vegetables, fruit and 'green stuff' (like watercress, chickweed, groun'sel – your five-a-day!), blacking, lucifers, corn-salves, grease-removing compositions, plating-balls, poison for rats, detonating-balls, dog-collars, birdcages, red-herring-toasters, boot-and stay-laces, shirt-buttons, snuff-boxes, pin-cushions, second-hand goods, live animals (like dogs, squirrels, and tortoises), handmade goods (like clothes-pegs, bonnet-boxes, rush baskets) . . . oh, whatever you wished was available *somewhere*.

A costermonger's best friend

A costermonger's donkey was close to his heart – sometimes it ate more than a member of his own family! And it could pull his cart anything from two to ten miles a day.

DID YOU KNOW?

* A costermonger's boy earned about 1/6 to 2 shillings a week.
* The cost of feeding a donkey would be about four- or fivepence a day, made up of a peck of chaff which costs 1d, a quart of oats and a quart of beans, each costing a penny halfpenny, and sometimes a pennyworth of hay.

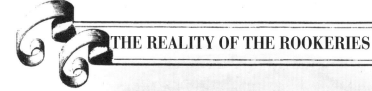

THE REALITY OF THE ROOKERIES

When you think about it, London ain't really all that big: a square mile of courts and lanes and alleys, surrounded by more streets and more people. My home patch, blackened by smoke and shrouded in a peasouper as it might be, is still home. And the rookeries – where pretty much everybody who's a nobody lives – is a place where I know everybody and everybody knows me (especially if I have any specie to hand). A Gospel-man once told me that God watches everything. Well, He'd probably see more than He'd want to if he took a gander at the underbelly of London.

In Dodger's London there was no safety net for those who fell – and when someone did fall, they could fall a very long way and were unlikely to bounce back, especially if they fell into the kind of midden and filth that coated the streets far away from the 'harristocratic' areas.

DID YOU KNOW?

✳ Slums were known as *rookeries*, as the jam of houses was similar to the way actual rooks built their habitats and lived communally.

✳ The term was first used in print in 1792 by a poet, George Galloway, who described a rookery as being 'a cluster of mean tenements densely populated by people of the lowest class'.

✳ The East London working class was a diverse mix of the native English with Irish immigrants, and those from Central and Eastern Europe – mostly Russian, Polish and German Jews.

✳ Seven Dials was a particularly notorious rookery, named after a seven-faced sundial at the junction of seven streets.

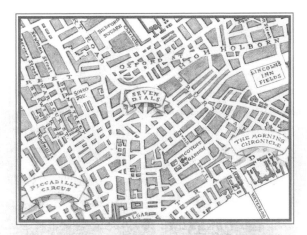

Mister Charlie Dickens – friend to the young Dodger – used his experiences in the rookeries in many of his novels. He once set out to explore the area known as Rat's Castle accompanied by a chief inspector of Scotland Yard and four other policemen, with more police within easy whistling distance in case of any trouble!

'Where is there such another maze of streets, courts, lanes, and alleys? Where such a pure mixture of Englishmen and Irishmen, as in this complicated part of London? The stranger who finds himself in 'The Dials' for the first time, and stands at the entrance of seven obscure passages, uncertain which to take, will see enough around him to keep his curiosity and attention awake for no inconsiderable time. From the irregular square into which he has plunged, the streets and courts dart in all directions, until they are lost in the unwholesome vapour which hangs over the house-tops, and renders the dirty perspective uncertain and confined . . .'

– Extract from *Sketches by Boz* by Charles Dickens (1836)

It can be a bit grubby down some streets. A few dead dogs, dead old lady maybe, but well, that's the way of the world, right? Like it says in the Good Book, you got to eat a peck of dirt before you die, right?

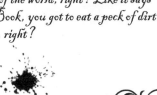

—— ·❧ Houses and Lodgings ❧· ——

Home is where your family is . . .

And quite possibly everyone else's as well, since a typical lodging house meant that a neighbour really *was* your neighbour – rubbing shoulder to shoulder against you. And any little friends he might be harbouring about his person would quickly become your little friends too, taking up residence in your armpits or crotch until you could pass them on. Especially when the lodging house ran a relay system where one person got a bed by day, and another had the same bed by night.

'A nice flock-bed for the boys . . .'

Whole families shared rooms with other families, or rented an extra bed out to children so they could 'slape aisy and comfortable'. Sixteen or more families might live in one building, in rooms above cow-sheds, donkey stables and workshops, with cartloads of refuse left in the yard and stagnant water in the streets.

DID YOU KNOW?

❧ By 1854, London had around 1,400 lodging houses with a total population of 30,000 – another 50,000 lived in known unregistered houses.

❧ Mister Henry Mayhew told Dodger how he once met a minister of a small church who had found 29 people in one apartment – when he knelt between two beds to pray for a dying woman, his legs became so jammed he could barely get up again!

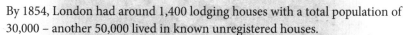

'Ladies and gentlemen were induced to don common clothes and go out in the highways and byways to see people of whom they had heard, but of whom they were as ignorant as if they were inhabitants of a strange country' – *New York Times* (1884)

And the bravest tourists might even spend a night in a poor lodging-house, eager to experience the closest associations with the lower classes. Some may have taken a bit more back with them than a memory . . .

For the itinerant pedlar or the cove down on his luck, fourpence or sixpence could buy a space to kip and a bite to eat in a flophouse – which could have as many as 40 rooms holding beds for 200 people. The kitchen might hold 400 people at once.

'When a man's lost caste in society, he may as well go the whole hog, bristles and all, and a low lodging-house is the entire pig' – a once-prosperous occupant of a flophouse, quoted in *London Labour and the London Poor*

'I was told by one trustworthy man that not long ago he was compelled to sleep in one of the lowest (as regards cheapness) of the lodging-houses. All was dilapidation, filth, and noisomeness. In the morning he drew, for purposes of ablution, a basinfull of water from a pailfull kept in the room. In the water were floating alive, or apparently alive, bugs and lice, which my informant was convinced had fallen from the ceiling . . .' – Henry Mayhew, *London Labour and the London Poor*

·❧ The Spectre of The Workhouse . . . ❧·

'Hush-a-bye baby, on the tree top,
When you grow old, your wages will stop,
When you have spent the little you made
First to the Poorhouse and then to the grave.'
– Anonymous verse

If you fell *too* far, often dragging your family along with you, then the workhouse awaited. Any destitute individual or family who couldn't scrape together the few pennies a night needed for a flophouse, and so otherwise faced shivering in a doorway or hunkering down under a bit of old tarpaulin, could get shelter and food in return for labour. And a fair dollop of God-thanking too, with prayers read to the paupers before breakfast and after supper, so that each unfortunate could reflect on God's Great Mercy in allowing a bed in a dormitory, away from their missus and children, with a nibble of cheese and a mouthful of bread in return for a couple of hours' work . . .

DID YOU KNOW?

 If you turned up at the doors with a lot of happy little friends crawling over your body, you might find yourself in a special 'foul' or 'itch' ward.

 Charlie Chaplin spent time with his mother in a workhouse in South London.

 In the 1840s, workhouse paupers fought over rotting bones they were crushing for fertilizer – they were so hungry they wanted to suck all the marrow out first!

 Breaking rules led to punishments – purposely smashing a window could mean two months in prison.

After 1845, Christmas Day was celebrated with roast beef, plum pud and a pint of porter.

Workhouse rules

Orders were issued after 1834 which listed 233 rules about running a workhouse, including the following:

WORK HOUSE RULES

ANY PAUPER WHO SHALL NEGLECT TO OBSERVE SUCH OF THE REGULATIONS HEREIN CONTAINED AS ARE APPLICABLE TO AND BINDING ON HIM:-

- Or who shall make any noise when silence is ordered to be kept
- Or shall use obscene or profane language
- Or shall by word or deed insult or revile any person
- Or shall threaten to strike or to assault any person
- Or shall not duly cleanse his person
- Or shall refuse or neglect to work, after having been required to do so
- Or shall pretend sickness
- Or shall play at cards or other games of chance
- Or shall enter or attempt to enter, without permission, the ward or yard appropriated to any class of paupers other than that to which he belongs
- Or shall misbehave in going to, at, or returning from public worship out of the workhouse, or at prayers in the workhouse
- Or shall return after the appointed time of absence, when allowed to quit the workhouse temporarily
- Or shall wilfully disobey any lawful order of any officer of the workhouse

—— SHALL BE DEEMED DISORDERLY ——

—— •❧ Earning a Living in the Rookeries ❧• ——

'The means resorted to in order to "pick up a crust", as the people call it, in the public thoroughfares (and such in many instances it *literally* is), are so multifarious that the mind is long baffled in its attempts to reduce them to scientific order or classification' – Henry Mayhew, *London Labour and the London Poor*

Noses to the grindstones, not to mention ears, teeth and even heads . . .

Street sellers, buyers, finders, performers, artisans and labourers, errand-boys, kids doing tricks, and the ever-present beggars . . . all life (well, all the life that is made up of thousands of nobodies) was out on the London streets. Scavengers, nightmen, flushermen, dustmen, crossing-sweepers, lighters and waterers, bill-stickers, horse-holders, shoe-blacks, street-porters . . . all ducking and diving, dodging and bobbing, dipping and weaving about the streets in order to pick up their crusts – or, if Lady Luck was with them, perchance enough to make a sandwich!

Manure means money

For the price of a broom – about twopence halfpenny – myriad crossing sweepers were at their posts morning to night, making sure no nobby traveller alighting from a growler ever stood in what the horse in front of said growler might have deposited on the street. A shilling a day might be their reward. And their patches were fiercely guarded . . .

Nutting potatoes for threepence a time . . .

Take one bag of large raw potatoes.
Add one man with a bald head.
Chuck threepence in the ring . . .
. . . and up goes the tatur!
Smashing into the man's head, the big raw tatur is shattered into a dozen pieces . . .

'Now chuck fourpence in,' says the exhibitor, 'and we'll see what we can do with a tatur just as large again!'

'There are blue bumps, and bumps of a faded greenish hue, and bumps red and inflamed, and his bald sconce looks as though it had been out in a rain of spent bullets . . .'

– Victorian gentleman on viewing the display

·❧ Ne'er-Do-Wells ❧·

'God bless you, sir, you truly are a gentleman, sir . . .'

Old sweats who marched to war with two legs and left one with Boney . . .

Ancient ladies missing not only most of their teeth but also a family – old ladies being fairly endemic, given that their husbands tended to head off to meet their Maker before they did . . .

Kids screwing up their fists to make their eyes water and bring forth better tears – tears full of real *soul* . . .

Whole families beseeching passers-by to help them feed their child'en afore the hungry Staggers made them all fall to the ground . . .

Beggars all, and each one aiming to avoid being the lead character in a cornoner's inquest.

Amazingly, every now and again you came across nobby folks who actually cared about the street people and were slightly guilty about them. If you were poor, and perhaps took the trouble to scrub up as best you could, and had no shame at all and could also spin a hard luck story, why, then they would practically kiss you, because it made them feel better.

(But a kiss buttered no parsnips, so the kiss had to come with some specie too.)

'We fear [the rookeries] for what they are; beds of pestilence, where the fever is generated which shall be propagated to distant parts of the town; rendezvous of vice . . . they are not only the haunts where pauperism recruits its strength – not only the lurking-places, but the *nurseries* of felons. A future generation of thieves is there hatched from the viper's egg.'
– Extract from *The Rookeries of London* by Thomas Beames (1852)

Henry Mayhew catalogued a list of ne'er'-do-wells in *Those That Will Not Work*, the Fourth Volume of *London Labour and the London Poor* (1861):

A COMPENDEUM OF THIEVES, CHEATS, BEGGERS, SCOUNDRALS ETC., THEIR METHODS REVEALED, SOCITAL CAUSES EXAMINED, AND PREVENTIVE MEASURES EXPLAINED. [sic]

BEGGARS AND CHEATS

Ladies and gentleman are warned to be particularly on the lookout for the following classes of unsavoury, dangerous and undeserving sorts of individuals:

BEGGING LETTER-WRITERS Foremost among beggars, by right of pretention to blighted prospects and correct penmanship.

DECAYED GENTLEMAN

The conversation of this class of mendicant is of former greatness, of acquaintance among the nobility and gentry of a particular county – always a distant one from the scene of operations . . . the cause of his ruin he attributes usually to a suit in the Court of Chancery, or the 'fatal and calamitous Encombured Irish Estates Bill'. He is a florid imposter and has a jaunty sonorous way of using his lean, threadbare, silk pocket-handkerchief, that carries conviction even to the most sceptical.

THE BROKEN-DOWN TRADESMAN

The broken-down tradesman is a sort of retail dealer in the same description of article as the decayed gentleman. The unexpected breaking of fourteen of the most respectable banking-houses in New York, or the loss of the cargoes of two vessels in the late autumnal gales, or the suspension of payment of Haul, Strong, and Chates, 'joined and combined together with the present commercial crisis, has been the means of bringing him down to his deplorable situation,' as his letter runs. He has a wife whose appearance in itself is a small income. She folds the hardest-working-looking set of hands across the cleanest of aprons, and curtseys with the humility of a pew-opener.

ASHAMED BEGGARS

By the above title I mean those tall, lanthorn-jawed men, in seedy well-brushed clothes who, with a ticket on their breasts, on which a short but piteous tale is written in the most respectable of large-hand, and with a few boxes of lucifer matches in their hands, make no appeal by word of mouth, but invoke the charity of passers-by by meek glances and imploring looks – fellows who, having no talent for 'patter' are gifted with great powers of facial pathos, and make expression of feature stand in lieu of vocal supplication...

CLEAN FAMILY BEGGAR

Beggars of this class group themselves artistically. A broken-down-looking man, in the last stage of seediness, walks hand-in-hand with a pale-faced, interesting little girl. His wife trudges on his other side, a baby in arm; a child just able to walk steadies itself by the hand that is disengaged; or other children cling about the skirts of her gown, occasionally detaching himself or herself – as a kind of rear or advanced guard from the main body – to cut off stragglers and pounce upon falling halfpence, or look piteously into the face of a passer-by.

The clothes of the whole troop are in that state when seediness is dropping into rags; but their hands and faces are perfectly clean – their skins literally shine – perhaps from the effect of a plentiful use of soap. The complexions of the smaller children, in particular, glitter like sandpaper, and their eyes are half-closed, and their noses corrugated, as with constant and compulsory ablution. The baby is a wonderful specimen of washing and getting-up of ornamental linen. Altogether, the Clean Family Beggars form a most attractive picture for quiet and respectable streets, and 'pose' themselves for the admiration of the thrifty matrons, who are their best supporters.

Sometimes the children of the Clean Family Beggars sing – sometimes the father 'patters'. This morning a group passed my window, who both sang and 'pattered'. The mother was absent, and the eldest girls knitted and crochetted as they walked along.

When you've got to pick a pocket or two ...

When even the peelers trod carefully and not a single one would come into the rookeries on his own, then the mean streets of London were home to a lot of hatched vipers (along with rats and mice, fleas and lice, cockroaches and flies) – to a lot of chancers, a lot of little hands prepared to give a new home to any of your possessions that you might not be aware you no longer had need of – a literal *army* of street kids so famously depicted in Mister Charlie Dickens's novel *Oliver Twist*.

A criminal vocabulary

To erase the original name or number from a stolen watch, and substitute one that is fictitious – **christening Jack.**

To take the works from one watch, and case them in another – **churching Jack.**

One who steals from the shopkeeper while pretending to effect an honest purchase – **a bouncer.**

One who entices another to play at a game at which cheating rules, such as card or skittle sharping – **a buttoner.**

To commit burglary – **crack a case, or break a drum.**

A thief who robs cabs or carriages by climbing up behind, and cutting the straps that secure the luggage on the roof – **a dragsman.**

Breaking a square of glass – **starring the glaze.**

To rob a till – **pinch a bob.**

A person marked for plunder – **a plant.**

Going out to steal linen in process of drying in gardens – **going snowing.**

Bad money – **sinker.**

Passer of counterfeit coins – **smasher.**

Stolen property generally – **swag.**

To go about half naked to excite compassion – **on the shallow.**

Coiners of bad money – **bit fakers.**

Midnight prowlers who rob drunken men – **bug hunters.**

Entering a dwelling house while the family have gone to church – **a dead lurk.**

Forged bank notes – **queer screens.**

– Extracted from *The Seven Curses of London* by James Greenwood (1869)

Geezerdom – 'No problem, 'nuff said, guv'nor, right you are.'

A king of geezering was Dodger himself. He wore the streets not just like an overcoat, but like a part of his own grubby skin. He was an actor, always playing the game, and if he went onto another man's patch he made sure to strut with the full swagger of the geezer. And with a nod and a wink and a gesture or two, he would make it known that he respected their patch whilst on it. And in return, they would surely offer him the same respect should they venture into Seven Dials. But just in case they didn't, well, he'd have his brass knuckles ready . . .

Every lad wants to be thought of as a wide boy, a geezer, right?

Gangs

But with young toughs prepared to give a knuckle sandwich or worse to anyone heading into their territory, the trouble could spill over into awful violence . . .

THE CLERKENWELL SHOOTING CASE

Dr. Danford Thomas held an inquiry on Saturday at St. Pancras into the death of Margaret Jane Smith . . . Alfred Smith, carman, deposed that while he was in Margaret-street, Clerkenwell, at nine on Thursday night, he noticed a gang of boys and girls – about 20 altogether – behaving in a very disorderly manner. A greengrocer's boy, named Joseph Steadman, was wheeling a barrow along the street when a lad named Mark quarrelled and fought with him. A girl shouted to a lad, 'Baker, fire,' and then the witness say Baker fire a revolver [sic] in the direction of the combatants. Witness's belief was that the shot was meant for Steadman. As soon as Baker fired witness saw the deceased girl fall. She was crossing the road between two gangs of boys.

Inspector Briggs said there were two gangs at feud. At Christmas the police arrested 28 of the lads, on some of whom revolvers were found. The fights between the gangs were renewed on Thursday night. The real name of the lad known as 'Baker' was Robson. He knew that he carried a revolver. One of the gangs belonged to Chapel-street, and the other to Margaret-street, Clerkenwell. Whenever one of the former came across one of the latter a fight ensued. Most of the Chapel-street gang carried revolvers. They discharged them when they entered Margaret-street to denote their approach. The fights generally originated in quarrels about girls.

– *Morning Post* (7 June 1897)

The unwary cove

Venturing into the alleys and courts of the East End, any stranger might expect to discover himself a possible victim of pickpockets, plus any number of *tea leaves* (thieves), who would be ready to nick a turnip off a stall, the laces out of your boots – or a shiny coin unwise enough to be looking for an adventure beyond its owner's pocketbook.

Other criminals to whom an unwary visitor could fall prey included:

- **Duffers and horse-chanters** – who sold poor goods or horses and cheated the buyer.
- **Charley pitchers** – gamblers who cheated.
- **Bouncers and besters** – who cheated by laying bets the punter could never win (such as the handy pea-under-a-thimble game).
- **Cracksmen** – who broke into houses.
- **Rampsmen** – who stopped people on the highways and robbed them.
- **Drummers** – who stole off those they had plied with liquor.
- **Bug-hunters** – who were on the lookout for drunks to rob.
- **Buzzers** – who picked gentlemen's pockets.
- **Wirers** – who aimed for ladies' pockets, and often had long thin fingers.
- **Thumble screwers** – who stole people's watches.
- **Drag-sneaks** – who stole from carts or coaches.
- **Garrotters** – street robbers.
- **Woolly bird stealers** – who stole sheep.

DID YOU KNOW?

Even the hair in horses' tails could be stolen and sold, with horsehair being worth 10d a pound. When two horsekeepers in an omnibus yard were caught selling the hair from their charges, the company was angrier about the fact that the horses' tails had been disfigured than they were about the value of the hair.

The Great Garrotting Panic of 1862 ...

When an MP was robbed in the street – 'garrotted' – on his way home from the Commons, the press (especially *The Times*, which wanted stricter sentences for criminals) fuelled a citywide panic, despite the number of victims actually being quite few (32 incidents in November was the worst). But the fearful gentleman heading out after dark could now buy special anti-garrotte collars and life-preservers lined with lead.

But an unwary cove was still a mark in a carriage, and even in their own home ...

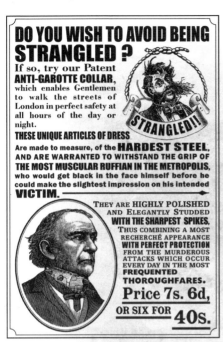

DO YOU WISH TO AVOID BEING STRANGLED ?

If so, try our Patent **ANTI-GAROTTE COLLAR**, which enables Gentlemen to walk the streets of London in perfect safety at all hours of the day or night.

THESE UNIQUE ARTICLES OF DRESS

Are made to measure, of the **HARDEST STEEL**, AND ARE WARRANTED TO WITHSTAND THE GRIP OF **THE MOST MUSCULAR RUFFIAN IN THE METROPOLIS**, who would get black in the face himself before he could make the slightest impression on his intended **VICTIM.**

THEY ARE HIGHLY POLISHED AND ELEGANTLY STUDDED **WITH THE SHARPEST SPIKES,** THUS COMBINING A MOST RECHERCHÉ APPEARANCE **WITH PERFECT PROTECTION** FROM THE MURDEROUS ATTACKS WHICH OCCUR EVERY DAY IN THE MOST **FREQUENTED THOROUGHFARES.**

Price 7s. 6d,

OR SIX FOR **40s.**

– Based on advertisement in *Punch* (1856)

'Among the many thieves who infest the London streets none are more artful or more active than the carriage thieves. No vehicle should ever be left with open windows; and valuable rugs in victorias, &c., should always be secured to the carriage by a strap or other fastening. Ladies should be especially careful of officious persons volunteering to open or close carriage doors. In nine cases out of ten these men and boys are expert pickpockets.'
– Extract from *Dickens's Dictionary of London* by Charles Dickens Jr. (1879)

SCENE.—*The Kitchen.*
Cook. "WHO WAS THAT AT THE DOOR, MARY !"
Mary. "OH ! SUCH A NICE-SPOKEN GENTLEMAN WITH MOUSTARSHERS. HE'S A WRITIN A LETTER IN THE DRAWING-ROOM. HE SAYS HE'S A OLD SCHOOLFELLER OF MASTER'S JUST COME FROM INGIA."

SCENE.—*The Hall.*
THE NICE-SPOKEN GENTLEMAN IS SEEN DEPARTING WITH WHAT GREAT-COATS AND OTHER TRIFLES HE MAY HAVE LAID HIS HANDS UPON.

Snakesmen: the master thieves

⊞ **Snakesman – WANTED** ☾

Qualities needed: skinny, agile lad needed with a head for heights (possibly supported by a hemp noose if he were to be sloppy or careless at his work).

Apply in person at   *Today or tomorrow*
Billies Booth, Seven Dials.   *at 9 pm of the clock.*

The *snakesman* was a thief who could shimmy up any drainpipe and into any crib – over the roof, through an open window, a fast slip in through a back door or a wriggle through a fanlight. Dodger himself had once seen fit to participate in this particular line of work with a certain success (a success that, surprisingly, drew the attention of Those Higher Up who later on could offer him a Very Advantageous New Position that involved these very skills).

> Snakesman! That had been fun, when he was a kid with his arse half out of his trousers, and because he was sharp and cleverer than the other brats, little skinny Dodger had been the king of snakesmen, able to get into tight places, scramble up to half-open fanlight windows and slither into and through tight spaces that a grown man could never get into. Then all he had to do was crack the lock on the nearest street door and let the burglars scurry in. For this errand he would get paid the princely sum of sixpence and a decent meal . . .

The tools of his trade

If the snakesman didn't want to end up dancing the Newgate jig, he needed to be able to ply his trade as quickly as possible. Dodger – like all snakesmen – had his special little bag of tricks, including:

* A **torsion wrench** – shaped like an L, this applied torque to the plug of a lock. Some, called feather-touch wrenches, had a coiled spring at the bend of the L.
* A **couple of half-diamond picks** – to pick individual pins. Dodger would take as many as three with him if the crib was a difficult bust.
* A **hook pick** – the tip shaped like a hook, used for raking.
* A **ball pick** – with a circular shape at the end.
* A **rake pick** – like the common snake rake – to slide past all the pins and bounce them about. It was the beginner's tool and the easiest way to crack a lock, but sometimes that was all a cheap lock needed.

The Great Social Evil

Stepping off the boat in Wapping Dock, or alighting from a coach up from the country, many innocent young girls found their dreams of a New Life in Glorious London shattered as the back slums of Whitechapel sucked them in and spat them out again, usually decked out in the garb of a naughty lady.

THE GREAT SOCIAL EVIL.

TIME :—Midnight.   A Sketch not a Hundred Miles from the Haymarket.

Bella. " AH ! FANNY ! HOW LONG HAVE YOU BEEN *GAY !*"*

*'Gay' in Victorian days meant being a naughty lady, not a naughty lady liking other naughty ladies.

'I was innocent once. But it didn't do me no good. Then I found out what I was doing wrong. But I was born on the streets here, knew what to expect. Them poor little innocents never stand a chance when the first kind gentleman plies them with liquor' – *Messy Bessie*

Dona Britannica Hollandia, the Arch-Mistris of the wicked women

Head and shoulders above most others in the area, Mrs Holland – herself a lady of 'ill reporte' – had the following to help protect the naughty ladies in her establishment:

* A portcullis, moat and wicket so that no one could sneak up, in – or indeed, out – without specie changing hands.
* A big hulking man on the door to quell disagreeable intruders.
* A handy riverside setting for any visitors meeting with misadventure (or who fancied a nice long trip across the seas to interesting countries).

DID YOU KNOW?

Many women turned to the work out of the need to make money. In Dodger's time there were about 50,000 girls working as naughty ladies in London – that's about one for every 20 adult men.

Soiled Doves?

Do-gooders, mostly with a Christian bent, headed for London's bridges as the light fell, especially on the lookout for girls driven to the bridges by despair (or an expanding waistline). The lucky girls often just got a leaflet and were urged not to sin any more, but as only the workhouse beckoned, sometimes the river still beckoned more.

'If that gal ain't watched this night, she is jest as likely to go to London Bridge and throw her blessed body hoff into the dirty water as not. They always go to Lunnun Bridge when they want to make way with themselves – it's so lively like' – policeman talking of a young lady who is 'fly to heverythink', from *Palace and Hovel: Phases of London Life* by Daniel Joseph Kirwan (1878)

When I was a kid, with the arse hanging out of me britches (no unmentionables for the likes of me) and a gnawing ache in my guts, I was just one of an army of urchins on the streets, ready to rush forward to hold a horse or sell on something I'd dug out of the muck. And when life pisses on you – or worse – well, you just have to make something out of the worse! Take a walk around and see the street kids now, eyes sharp, full of guile and mischief, but if the opportunity arises also ready to pick up a penny or two. Or ready to pick up the richards falling like manna from heaven from under the tails of the shire horses pulling the carts – valuable bounty that can then be sold by the bucket around the nobbier districts for their gardens. You would always hear them shouting in the street, 'Tuppence a bucket, well stamped down'. And, God help me, there was the rag and bone men, and not just rags and bones either. And that's the shape of it. In good old London everything has a price, even the soot – you don't think so? Best export from the city is your soot. The farmers take it away in their carts, it being good for the land, you see. And bless me, some people forge soot out of any old dust as long as it's dark, but even that dust has worth if it comes out of somebody's house. Every little thing has a price in this city and you'll see old girls with their chafed knees sifting the dust looking for any bit of metal. In London anything or anyone is for sale.

Street children were everywhere, doing whatever was necessary to get a pie in the belly by the end of the day:

- Selling stuff . . .
- Working as errand boys, bootblacks, handing out playbills or advertising . . .
- Hired as toddlers by beggars who had no children of their own to draw more pity from the charitable . . .
- Doing tricks like standing on their hands as an omnibus went by so that passengers could throw down pennies in appreciation . . .
- Accosting a nobby pedestrian with an offer to entertain them . . .
- Holding horses . . .
- Or sweeping the streets . . .

DID YOU KNOW?

Foundlings taken into orphanages were often given names in alphabetical order – no matter how daft the name sounded. Hence Dodger himself had once gone by the moniker of Master Pip Stick (a name that did a lot to teach him how to use his fists).

———·❧ Girls ☙·———

Throughout the busy streets, especially in the nobby areas around theatres or public houses, the cries of young girls rang out as they hawked fruit, flowers and cresses from baskets, buying their stock early at Covent Garden and selling on at a profit of as much as sixpence a day, if Lady Luck was holding their hand.

A little mother in training

When a girl was big enough, she'd find herself looking after her family's littler children – or she might even get lent out to help carry a baby about (if a handy old lady hadn't already cornered that particular market, since old ladies didn't get to be old without also getting to be a bit cunning, and it was amazing how fast the old girls could move at the prospect of sixpence a week). And for a girl, what was the use of an education? It wouldn't 'yarn a gal a living'.

And Mum herself might be a bit the worse for wear . . .

"THE CLEW."

The Child was evidently lost!—cried bitterly—could not tell us where its Parents lived, or whether she was an Orphan, or what her Father was—or where she went to School.——Enter Intelligent Policeman.

Policeman (in a friendly whisper). "WHERE DOES YOUR MOTHER GET HER GIN, MY DEAR?" [*And the mystery was solved!*

·❧ Mudlarks ❧·

Was a mudlark for a while first, 'cos, well, that's the kind of stuff you like as a kid – it sort of comes natural, if you know what I mean, mucking about in the river mud picking up bits of coal and suchlike. Not bad in the summer, bloody awful in the winter . . .

The bounty of the river

The gifts from the retreating tide were picked over by daily hordes of mudlarks, clad in rags with the foul soil of the Thames coating their grimy bodies.

ON THE THAMES AT LOW WATER.

A wealth of waste

The ends of smoked cigars were known as 'hard-ups' – finders could dry out the tobacco in these and either smoke or sell it. Some mudlarks even collected dog poo, which could be sold to tanneries to be used in the production of leather goods.

DID YOU KNOW?

 Mudlarks were mostly kids but there were also old women with their backs bent over through age or illness, carefully sifting among the wet mud for little bits of coal, or any rubbish that might be worth a penny or two.

 From Execution Dock in Wapping down to Limehouse Hole there were 14 different sets of stairs or landing-places where mudlarks could get down to the shore.

 At popular sets of stairs, there might be as many as 40 or 50 mudlarks working on any one day.

 Mudlarks often ended up in prison for petty thefts, but many found it more comfortable than everyday life!

Working on the river wasn't plain sailing

'About two year ago I left school, and commenced to work as a mudlark on the river . . . picking up pieces of coal and iron, and copper, and bits of canvas on the bed of the river, or of wood floating on the surface . . . When the bargemen heave coals to be carried from their barge to the shore, pieces drop into the water among the mud, which we afterwards pick up . . . The mudlarks are generally good swimmers. When a bargeman gets hold of them in his barge on the river, he often throws them into the river, when they swim ashore and take off their wet clothes and dry them. They are often seized by the police in the middle of the river, and thrown overboard, when they swim to the shore. I have been chased twice by a police galley' – eleven-year-old mudlark to Henry Mayhew, *London Labour and the London Poor*

According to a report in *The Era* on 11 July 1841, one notorious female mudlark regularly took scavenging a little too far when she stole coal from barges moored on the river. She dropped the coal into the river and smeared it in mud to make it look as if she had found it on the foreshore. When the river police would try to arrest her, she would resist and roll around in the mud, determined to make them as dirty as she was.

BREAD, GREASE, A PIE AND A PINT

For me and my chums, as we grew up, a belly full of food was always the reward for a good day's begging, stealing, or – if all else failed – earning. And did it really matter if the meat in the pie had a bit of what you might call a dubious origin? Though Solomon was very strict about not eating anything too dodgy – so I did tend to draw the line at eating anything that I'd have to nail down to stop it from actually running away. But it's amazing what some people fake. You gots fake oranges and even fake bananas, all looking nice when they're sold, and tomorrow, why, you'll never recognize the cove that sold them to you.

DID YOU KNOW?

* Most of the nobodies Dodger knew lived on tea and bread, or bread and grease with the occasional herring as a real treat.
* For a married couple doing well, dinner might include 'good block ornaments' – bits of meat like tripe or cow heels.
* A lot of street folk preferred the beer shop to going home at night.
* Beer cost about threepence a pot (two pints), if you brought your own jug.

Codswallop!

Where did the phrase 'It's a load of old codswallop' come from? A bottle. In the 1880s, inventor Hiram Codd designed a new type of bottle for fizzy mineral water. In the neck of the Codd's bottle was a washer and a marble, and when the bottle was filled up with the 'wallop', the gas in the water would push the marble into the water and seal the contents. And when it was empty, why, a lot of fun could be had with the marbles after the bottles were broken.

Dodger himself ate better than most, as his mentor Solomon had the remarkable ability to take a bit of old beef as tough as shoe-leather, add a few vegetables and turn up a pot of delights. The old man never told Dodger much about his travels, but all that wandering through wildernesses had certainly made him able to do the best with what he could pick up (possibly at a run, since Solomon had been wont to cross countries at a decent rate of knots). He had also learned how to be *adaptable* about the rules of being Jewish . . .

However, what might be *in* your food *was* a concern worthy of note:

In an eating establishment . . .

"SEVERE."

Dainty Old Gent. "HAVE I LIKED MY DINNER?—NO, I'VE NOT! SO DON'T GIVE WHAT I'VE LEFT TO THE CAT, SIR; BECAUSE AS SHE'S SURE TO BECOME PIE, I SHOULD LIKE HER TO DIE A NATURAL DEATH, AND NOT BE POISONED."

At the door . . .

"Fresh, marm ! ! !   Why trouts feeds on insex, and the very flies fancies they're alive.   See how they hovers about 'em, just as if they was now a-swimming in the river."   [VERDICT—*Rayther stale.*

Or even in the shop . . .

THE USE OF ADULTERATION.

Little Girl. "IF YOU PLEASE, SIR, MOTHER SAYS, WILL YOU LET HER HAVE A QUARTER OF A POUND OF YOUR BEST TEA TO KILL THE RATS WITH, AND A OUNCE OF CHOCOLATE AS WOULD GET RID OF THE BLACK BEADLES"

A mummified heart for supper?

One Victorian eccentric, Dr William Buckland, became well known for some of the bizarre things he feasted upon – these included a meal of elephants' trunks, a tankard of bat's urine – and the mummified heart of King Louis XIV!

·❧ Food Stalls ❧·

Fancy an oyster washed down with some warm donkey's milk? What about a pickled whelk? If you were feeling peckish you could take your pick from fast-food stalls selling nosh such as hot eels, sheep's trotters, plum 'duff', muffins and crumpets. And Dodger and his friends would wash their grub down with ginger beer or – if really pushed – water.

Soup, glorious soup . . . a ladleful of exploration for only twopence!
Dodger had a very soft spot for Marie Jo, a lady once married to a Froggy (but he didn't think it fair to hold that against her) who now ran a soup stall open as regular as the peals of the Bow bells. And you could trust her soup . . .

All right, there may occasionally have been a bit of horse, that being the Froggy way, but it just meant you had a slightly more nourishing soup.

Baked taturs

- ❀ Potatoes were baked in large tins at the baker's, then taken in baskets to the stalls, where they were kept warm in tins over hot water.
- ❀ Some people with more specie than hunger would buy them in the winter just to keep their hands warm.
- ❀ Trade fell off when it was foggy as people couldn't see the potatoes properly and thought they might be rotten.

'Wen like the fog's like a cloud come down, people looks very shy at my taties, very; they've been more suspicious ever since the taty rot . . . Perhaps I make 12s or 15s a week – I hardly know, for I've only myself and keep no 'count for the season; money goes one can't tell how, and 'specially if you drinks a drop, as I do sometimes. Foggy weather drives me to it, I'm so worritted' – baked potato seller to Henry Mayhew, *London Labour and the London Poor*

Eel, beef or mutton pies! Penny pies, all 'ot – all 'ot!'

A pie has always been a mystery bag – as the pie-sellers themselves admitted. One man told Dodger's friend Mister Mayhew that 'People, when I go into houses, often begin crying, "Mee-yow," or "Bow-wow-wow!" at me.'

DID YOU KNOW?

 About three-quarters of a million pies were eaten on the streets every year.

 The pie shops did the street trade a lot of harm, as they made bigger pies for a penny than those sold in the street.

 A London pieman might average 8 shillings a week out of his pies.

Tossing the pieman – 'Here's all 'ot! Toss or buy! Up and win 'em!'

If the pennies had gone on beer, there was a way of winning a pie – tossing the pieman! If the pieman won the toss, then he earned his penny without handing over the pie; but if he lost then the cove won the pie. Coster boys – lads working on the street stalls selling fruit and veg – loved a gamble, and flash geezers often tossed when they didn't even want the pie. If they won it they just chucked it at one of their drinking friends – or at the pieman!

And if you fancied something a bit more nobby . . .

'Hot green peas are served in teacups at some outdoor establishments. The peculiarity of this form of light refreshment is the prodigality of the customers in the matter of vinegar and pepper, which are à discretion and gratis' – Extract from *Living London* by George R. Sims (1901)

This Little Piggy Went to Market...

Smithfield Market

More than a million pigs were sold at Smithfield Market annually, though weekly markets were mostly for cattle and sheep, with more than 220,000 head of cattle and 1,500,000 sheep a year forced through the narrow streets into the market.

Days:

Monday – Fat cattle and sheep.

Tuesday, Thursday and Saturday – Hay and straw.

Friday – Cattle and sheep; then scrub-horses and asses from 2 p.m. onwards.

DID YOU KNOW?

- Deals were done by shaking hands – and always for cash.
- The big event of the year was the great cattle show in December.
- The animals were crowded into any available space and there were lots of cruel practices, including 'pething' (hitting them over the horns) or 'hocking' (hitting them on the legs). Victorian campaigners worked to improve the conditions.

THE LAST DAY OF OLD SMITHFIELD MARKET.

Billingsgate Market

Salmon, cod, haddock, soles, mackerel, herrings, bloaters, eels, whiting, plaice, turbot, brill and mullet, oysters, crabs, lobsters, prawns and shrimps . . . the sheer quantities of fish brought in and sold at Billingsgate was astounding – enough for each Londoner to eat about two fish per day!

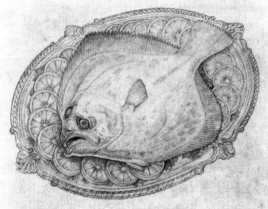

'What on earth becomes of the shells of five hundred million oysters, and the hard red coats of the eighteen hundred thousand lobsters and crabs?' – Victorian commentator, in *London Characters and the Humorous Side of Life* by W. S. Gilbert (c.1870)

DID YOU KNOW?

  The original name of Billingsgate was Blynesgate and then Byllynsgate – believed to refer to the owner of a gate where the goods were landed.

 It only began to specialize in fish in the 16th century.

The market was rebuilt in 1877 – it was twice as big as before, covering about 30,000 square feet with a glass roof.

 A special machine was installed to suck the foul air up through an air shaft and out into the sky – it used a centrifugal action and could carry out 50,000 feet of smelly, fishy air every minute!

·🎋 Slaking a Thirst – Beer and Water 🎋·

The stalls sold milks and ginger beers, but there was only one place for any geezer to go when he was thirsty – the public house. A pint of porter was often like a meal in itself, and although too much of it could make you fall over in the stinking street, it was far better than drinking water as that could make you fall stinking into the grave.

> 'He who drinks a tumbler of London Water has literally in his stomach more animated beings than there are Men, Women and Children on the face of the Globe' – *Sydney Smith, Anglican cleric*

FATHER THAMES INTRODUCING HIS OFFSPRING TO THE FAIR CITY OF LONDON
(A Design for a Fresco in the New Houses of Parliament.)

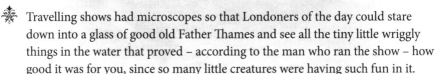

DID YOU KNOW?

🎋 Travelling shows had microscopes so that Londoners of the day could stare down into a glass of good old Father Thames and see all the tiny little wriggly things in the water that proved – according to the man who ran the show – how good it was for you, since so many little creatures were having such fun in it.

🎋 When Queen Victoria came to the throne only half of London's infants lived to their fifth birthday – many early deaths were due to cholera, spread in the water.

THE "SILENT HIGHWAY" - MAN.
"Your MONEY or your LIFE!"

When even the rats preferred the beer

If the bad news was that water wasn't good for your health, Dodger knew that the good news was that beer obviously was! Even the rats proved how big and strong beer could make you as the brewery rats were the biggest and fattest in the London sewers – the rat-catchers were paid more for them because they had such a lot of fight.

The great British pint

❁ In October 1814, in St Giles, England, a brewery tank filled with 3,500 barrels burst and a flood of beer roared down the streets, destroying two houses and leaving nine people dead (and probably quite a lot more dead drunk).

❁ It was quite common to have beer or wine with breakfast.

❁ 'On the wagon' is a popular term meaning to have stopped drinking anything alcoholic. But did you know that it came from the practice of allowing prisoners on their way to be hanged at Tyburn a last drink at a public house on their way? If anyone wanted to buy them a second drink, the guard would refuse, saying that the prisoner was going on the wagon.

Like most everyone else I knew, I grew up thinking of clobber just as something necessary, to keep me dry – warm too, if possible. If I wanted to look really flash, well, there was always the shonky shops, but Solomon then introduced me to a world of nobby schmutter and it was like a new world. A tailor might always be just a tailor, and the rest just shine, but it's a shine that is very shiny and says as 'This gent has got some specie!' And the unmentionables! Well, my crotch area certainly liked being among the gentry . . .

The nobbiest nobs had swanky establishments offering all the attire a gentleman might need – and these gentlemen treated the state of their clothing as a serious business . . .

DISTWESSING—VEWY.

X. 42. "DID YOU CALL THE POLICE, SIR?"

Swell (who would perish rather than disturb his shirt-collar). "YA-AS, A—I'VE HAD THE MISFORTUNE TO DWOP MY UMBRELLAW, AND THERE ISN'T A BOY WITHIN A MILE TO PICK IT UP—A—WILL YOU HAVE THE GOODNESS?"

A scrubbed-up Sol

A man who usually wandered around in embroidered slippers or old boots, and wore a ragged black gabardine, had suddenly become an old-fashioned but very smart gentleman with a fine black woollen barathea jacket, dark-blue pantaloon trousers and long, dark-blue woollen stockings with ancient but well-kept court shoes sporting silver buckles that shone . . .

The Wisdom of Solomon: 'Horse urine is, as we know, very good for cleaning clothes – a fact not everyone appreciates, though everybody knows it has a smell like good cider, and is very fruity.'

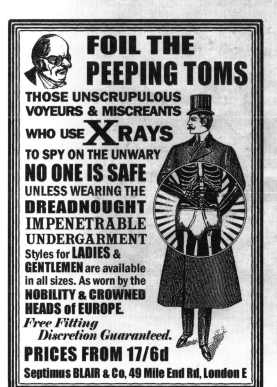

X-rayted unmentionables

Wilhelm Röntgen's discovery of X-rays in 1895 prompted widespread fear that this technology would be used by peeping Toms. Quick to capitalize, merchants began selling 'X-ray-proof underwear'.

> ### DID YOU KNOW?
> Some Victorian gentlemen used the bones from a badger's willy as a tie clip.

·❧ Shonky Shops ❧·

Not quite the full shilling

For the non-nobs, i.e. everyone else, clobber came much lower down the list of daily priorities – you can't eat a hat, after all (though people have tried to eat their boots). If a geezer wanted to look flash, well, that's what the dolly shops or shonky shops were for – unlicensed pawnshops and second-hand shops that could clothe you from head to foot in decent schmutter for the sum of about one shilling, including boots. Or less if Solomon Cohen was involved in the dealing.

The second-hand clothes trade was mostly run by the East End Jews – whole families of tailors sewing, mending, seaming and remodelling clothes that had been on the backs of up to four or five previous owners.

A hat for every head

Everybody wore a hat of some kind: a square hat for a printer, a leather cap for a tosher who didn't want to crack his skull open on a low tunnel, a reinforced hat for a peeler – and a skullcap for Solomon and his countrymen.

THE HOME & COLONIAL HAT COMPANY

'CROWNING' THE HEADS OF ENGLAND SINCE 1815

41 ALDGATE HIGH ST, LONDON, E

Props: Mr Abraham Leibowitz, Mr Harry Schmutter.

SILK & BEAVER 'TOPPERS' NEW FROM 10/6

REINFORCED 'PEELERS' AVAILABLE NEW & SECONDHAND.

NEW 'DERBY' FROM 5/-

NEW BOWLERS FROM 7/6

DERBIES, BOWLERS & 'CRUSHERS' IN ALL SIZES.

HOMBURGS & 'SOFTS' NEW FROM 3/6

BOATERS NEW FROM 2/-

BOYS & MENS CAPS FROM 1/-

'FINEST STEEL'

CAP 'COMFORTERS' & PROTECTIVES TO FIT ALL SIZES & STYLES.

FULL PROTECTIVES WITH EAR PIECES & SHARPENED BRIMS NEW & USED ALWAYS AVAILABLE. HYGIENICALLY CLEANED AND REPAIRED.

WE OFFER OUR ESTEEMED CLIENTELE A SERVICE SECOND TO NONE. ALL OUR HATS ARE FITTED ACCORDING TO THE PRINCIPLES OF PHRENOLOGY. DISCRETION GUARANTEED ON THE PURCHASE OF RESTORED HEADWEAR. MASONIC REGALIA & CLUBS CATERED FOR.

☞ **ALL STYLES, LATEST FASHIONS, NEW & RESTORED.** ☜

GETTING ABOUT

There's no doubting that the streets are a bit grubby. There are open sewers all over the place – and people not too particular either about what they chuck in 'em – and what with the horses everywhere (and we all know what horses like to leave behind), well, getting around can be a downright adventure for the unwary. Both a cap and a stout pair of boots are often a good idea when making shift down some of the alleys of the rookeries.

So much coal was burned in London chimneys that the yellow fogs, curling around the alleys and courts, made it virtually impossible at times to see where you were going. Even the rain fought a losing battle against the layers of dirt – mostly it just fought its way through the murkiness to put back on the street what the chimneys had taken away. A boon to the dips, a friend to the naughty ladies whose younger days had fled screaming many moons ago, the low-lying peasoupers meant that anyone could easily fall down a hole – or into the river.

—·❧ Two Wheels – a New-Fangled Way of Getting About ❧·—

Well, it certainly shook your bones about. A two-wheeled machine made of wood, with metal tyres, appeared on the London streets in 1865, and some of the nobbiest swells could be seen taking a turn around Hyde Park on what commonly became known as a 'boneshaker'. Particularly uncomfortable, so Dodger was informed, on cobblestones . . . Machines with solid rubber tyres turned up later, with the front wheels becoming larger and larger. It was named: the bicycle.

DID YOU KNOW?

❖ The first bicycles cost the equivalent of about six months' pay for a young man of modest income.

❖ The cyclist sat very high, and if the front wheel got stuck in a rut, they were likely to be tipped headfirst over the handlebars – this was the origin of the term 'taking a header'.

Preserving one's modesty

For the lady who was bold enough to take to two wheels, a bicycle was made available which had a special tilting saddle so that her dress would not be caught when mounting. A 'safety cycling skirt' could also be purchased from a limited number of tailors.

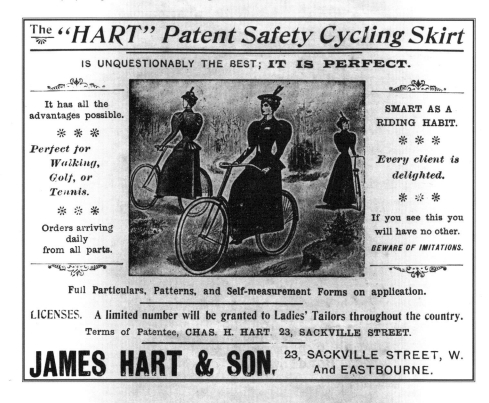

Watermen

Watermen were the cabbies of the Thames, plying their trade along the banks of the river, taking passengers across for a few pennies.

Money for corpses

The watermen also earned extra specie by picking bodies out of the river – they could gaff the corpse and row it down to the coroner of one of the boroughs, where they would collect a bounty for each body handed in.

Doggett's wager

Newly qualified watermen were able to prove their strength by entering the annual 'Doggett's Coat and Badge' race – a course of 4 miles and 5 furlongs from London Bridge to Chelsea. The winner got a much-prized red coat and silver badge. The race was first run in 1715 as a result of a will left by Thomas Doggett, a Drury Lane comedian, and is the oldest single-scull race in the world.

·❦ A Coach and Four ❦·

For long journeys – oh, as far away as Bristol – then a coach was the required form of transport. And the swankiest gents had their own coaches, often complete with crests and nobby coachmen.

But it was hard to beat a growler for a short journey. Driving a cab was generally reckoned to be an easy and exciting life for the working man, but cabbies worked very differing, and often long, hours:

- ❀ Long-day men were out for 16–20 hours a day. They usually got two horses, with a change of horse in the late afternoon.
- ❀ Morning men began around 7 a.m. and worked through to about 6 p.m. (so a bit more than a morning!). They had a one-horse-only setup.
- ❀ Short-night men worked from 6 p.m. through to 6 a.m.

✴ Bucks were unlicensed cabbies – mostly coves who had lost their licences through being the Worse for Drink, which was not generally considered a Good Idea when in charge of a horse and cab on a London thoroughfare. They hung around the cab stands looking for fill-in work, for instance when a long-day man grabbed the chance of a pie.

And, as ever, fares could be a matter of argument. Dodger himself once paid for a cab ride simply with his signature, and Solomon could bargain such a good deal that the cabbie would only recall it when Solomon was long gone.

AN UNREASONABLE COMPLAINT.

Indignant Party. "WHAT? A SHILLING FOR THE TWO MILES, AND A SIXPENCE BESIDES! WHY, YOU DON'T CALL ME AN EXTRA PERSON?"

Cabman. "OH! DON'T I THO'!"

> *The Wisdom of Solomon*: 'I have never really understood why these gentlemen seem so hostile to their clientele. You would have thought that driving a growler was a job for somebody who liked people, wouldn't you?'

A WASH AND A SCRUB

I used to reckon as that a bit of a splash of water on my face would be enough to get by, but the cove I lived with – old Sol – he made it very clear once I got a berth in his crib that a bit more scrubbing and so forth would be necessary if I was to share his living space. According to Sol, a bit of cleanliness was a step on the path of good health too, and as he was a gent who'd lived more than his fair share of years, and as one of the chosen people, I reckoned he was worth listening to. And there was no doubt that I could come out of the sewers after a stint of toshing with a rather . . . fruity . . . a-roma about my person.

A Roman Goddess

The London sewers were originally built by the Romans, chiefly to allow rainwater to find a way to get into the river. There were no toilets in the average home – chamber pots were emptied into the street (often onto some unfortunate's head) and cesspits took everything else. Or were supposed to . . .

These days toffs here and there were getting pipes run from their cesspits into the sewers . . . really unfair. It was bad enough with all the rats down here, without having to make certain you didn't step in a richard.

DID YOU KNOW?

Poor old Richard III's name made such a happy rhyme with an interesting word that a 'richard' became a common term for something you would rather not step in. It makes you wonder why Richard III was chosen, though. Why not Henry III, or Edward III?

Cloacina

The Romans had lots of gods and goddesses – and the goddess of the main drain of the city was Cloacina. Statues of her were found in the sewers and the Romans would pray to her to make sure going to the loo was a, er, smooth business.

'O Cloacina, Goddess of this place,
Look on thy suppliants with a smiling face.
Soft, yet cohesive let their offerings flow,
Not rashly swift nor insolently slow.'

Dodger, of course, knew Cloacina as the Lady. He had never seen her himself, but he knew what she looked like – every tosher did: a beautiful lady with a shiny dress and rat's claws on her feet. She was known to bite her favourites on the neck so that no other rats would harm them. And she would always be surrounded by her congregation – rats, rats and even more rats.

'Tread on a rat and you're treading on the Lady's robe' – *Toshers' saying.*

DID YOU KNOW?

 A rat's teeth are harder than iron.

 A rat can last longer without water than a camel.

 When many rats get tangled up by their tails, they can create what is known as a *rat king* – the largest ever found being a bunch of 32 mummified black rats discovered in a fireplace in Germany in 1828.

 Rats eat the equivalent of 10% of their body weight daily.

 A group of rats is called a mischief.

·❧ Bazalgette and the Great Stink ❧·

'Whoso once inhales the stink can never forget it,' as a newspaper of the day said of the river.

Summer 1858 – and the stench of London was up everybody's nose as a heat wave and drought made sure that *nothing* was washed away. As the nobs were suffering too (even Parliament had to be suspended) it was clear that Something Had to Be Done.

Joseph Bazalgette (1819–91) – a man with a moustache and a theodolite

Armed with his engineer's equipment, waterproof boots, expendable trousers – and the most spectacular bushy moustache – Joseph Bazalgette descended into the sewers (on one occasion with Dodger himself as his guide) and emerged to become chief engineer of the Metropolitan Commission of Sewers.

DID YOU KNOW?

 Bazalgette built five massive new sewers measuring 82 miles, hidden by embankments alongside the Thames and connected to existing sewers.

 To line the tunnels, he used 318 million bricks.

 3.5 million cubic yards of earth had to be dug up and shifted.

In total, Bazalgette built and repaired nearly 1,300 miles of sewers.

Your Country Needs You – to pee!

Bazalgette proposed to build public loos at key points throughout London and then collect and sell the pee – so everyone would pay a sort of 'pee tax' to help the economy.

To s(t)ink or swim

Imagine drowning in raw sewage! In September 1878, 800 people on board the *Princess Alice*, coming back from a jolly day out at the seaside, did just that as their ship collided with another boat at Barking just as two outfall pipes spurted out their sewage. For Bazalgette's sewers spat the stinky, lumpy sewage out into the river at Barking Reach, 20 miles from the sea (sadly for the people living alongside those 20 miles). The *Princess Alice* went down in this sludge in less than five minutes.

Don't like being in boats myself. Not good for you, all that water. Spend time toshing, you gets to not like too much water . . .

·❦ Hunting the Tosheroon ❦·

Down *under* the feet of London, toshers like Dodger crawled through the tunnels, looking for the glint of specie or jewellery amongst the muck. They navigated by experience, sometimes through smell alone . . . all for about six shillings a day – a good living in the rookeries, and hopefully enough for a tosher to buy himself a regular new pair of shonky trousers.

To Dodger, toshing wasn't work – toshing was *living*, and the sewers were among his favourite places, with names to match: the Maelstrom, the Queen's Bedroom, the Golden Maze, Sovereign Street, Button Back Spin, Breathe Easy, the Grotto and the Chamber of Whispers.

> ### DID YOU KNOW?
> The sewer tunnels were mostly only about 3 ft 9 inches high.

THE SEWER-HUNTER.

The tosher's dream

Fame? No. Fortune? Yes! For if you believed in the Lady and used all your skills, a tosher might one day be lucky enough to find the treasure at the end of the . . . rainbow-coloured sludge: the legendary *tosheroon*, which would have all that any tosher might need for the rest of his life. But if you offended the Lady, or got sloppy, you'd be more likely to come out of the sewers with a boot full of richards than a pocketful of gold.

> 'An interesting profession, but not one for a man hoping for a long life' – *Charlie Dickens to Dodger*
>
>
>
> 'Toshers die young; what else can you expect if you spend half your life messing about in mess? You never see a Jewish tosher, you can't be a kosher tosher!' – *Solomon*

To suffocate or starve?

Toshers mostly had two choices – they could scrabble around down below and make a living, or they could scrabble around down there and die. But when it became illegal after 1840 to go into the sewers without permission, toshers often moved on to night work: now they also went there in the dark to live or die. A reward for peaching a tosher was up for grabs too . . . and some liked to grab this handful of specie rather than root around for a handful of something else.

DID YOU KNOW?

 Toshers working at night-time often carried a dark lantern – they had a little door so you could shut off the light if you didn't want to be seen.

 Toshers are remembered today every time someone says, 'That's a load of old tosh', meaning something is rubbish.

Pigs in muck?

If it was bad enough dodging the reward-hunters and the rat-catchers, then worse awaited if an unlucky tosher ran into the ferocious pigs rumoured to haunt the tunnels in the north of the city – pigs that would eat *anything*. Luckily, however, any pig trying to get to Dodger's patch had to swim across the Fleet Ditch (a bricked-over river) – which they wouldn't do. It might have been fun to go and hunt for them, but on the other hand those things had big teeth and tusks!

──── ❦ Washing Off the Filth ❦ ────

The Wisdom of Solomon: 'Cleanliness is next to godliness . . .
but cleanliness gives godliness a run for its money.'

A wash in the river?

A dip in the Thames might have seemed like a good idea, but the bather might go in
there with grubby skin and come out with more than they bargained for – for the Thames
water harboured all the debris of London, including dead animals and the odd person.

THE LONDON BATHING SEASON.
"COME, MY DEAR!—COME TO ITS OLD THAMES, AND HAVE A NICE BATH!"

Or in a public park?

Mister Henry Mayhew was told how the sweeps' climbing boys used to be taken to
wash in the Serpentine in London's Hyde Park, but after one boy drowned, the children
preferred to keep their soot.

Or a trip to the public baths?

Where democracy truly reigned, as any Londoner could share their bath water (literally,
though not at the same time) with the nobbiest of coves. For the more you paid in a
London bathhouse, the hotter and cleaner the water – but it was still the *same* water.

Bath number 1 . . . for the nobs.
Bath number 2 . . . just a bit soapy, for the middle classes.
Bath numbers 3, 4, 5 etc. . . . for the great unwashed.

Turkish baths were particularly exciting – though sadly not as exciting as Dodger had hoped after hearing about them from his friend Ginny-Come-Lately, who had filled his mind with exciting images of dancing girls in very thin vests.

But the nobbiest of nobs would have their baths at home – filled by the effort of kitchenmaids, who had to heat the water down below, then haul it up to the bath, only to repeat the exercise in reverse when the bather had concluded their business.

Special baths were also available . . .

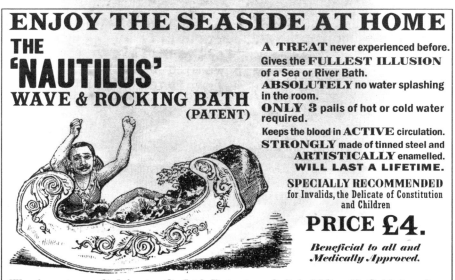

THE LONG ARM OF THE LAW

If there is one rule among the rookeries (and it's the sort of place where rules aren't liked very much), then it is this: you never peach to a policeman. And if you have to talk to one, well, it's amazing what a bit of memory loss can do to make your future less painful. You would certainly have seen nothing, done nothing, and probably not even been in the city on the day in question. No, the streets have their own kinds of justice and it doesn't involve no peeler in a hard hat trying to shove a body around. Oh, the peelers! At least the Bow Street Runners could be outrun, on account of them often being fat and full of grog, but the peelers, they will fight with them Cockneys. I mean, a fight between the peelers and the Cockney lads would be like that stuff that happened in Rome, which I believe is somewhere in Greece. No, you don't want a peeler on your tail, there's too many smart ones these days.

> *The Wisdom of Solomon*: 'I always think one should lie to policemen; it is so very good for the soul and, indeed, good for the policemen.'

⚜ Run from the Runners . . . ⚜

From the middle of the 18th century, thieves and crooks of all ilk in the East End ran the risk of being nabbed by a 'runner' – one of the officers of the new force known as the Bow Street Runners. Just like the old thief-takers, who solved petty crimes for a fee, the runners mostly got paid via rewards from the courts or victims, so any thief with his head screwed on knew that a pocketful of specie would keep a runner happy. And as for the petty crimes, well, Dodger himself ran foul of the runners, but what active young lad couldn't outrun a man who could see very little reward in apprehending an urchin?

I had a little difficulty concerning a stolen goose and got chased by the runners, just because I had feathers all over me, and so I hid out in the sewers, see? They didn't even follow, on account of being too fat and too drunk, in my opinion . . .

DID YOU KNOW?

- The Bow Street Runners force was founded in 1749 by Henry Fielding, author of *Tom Jones*, who was magistrate for Westminster and Middlesex at the time.
- After Henry died, his blind half-brother John succeeded him. Known as the 'Blind Beak of Bow Street', John allegedly had a heightened sense of hearing and was able to recognize 3,000 criminals by their voice.
- In Dodger's day, a horse patrol protected* London from highwaymen. The most notorious area was Hounslow Heath.

Everett and Bird robbing a Stage-Coach on Hounslow Heath.

*Well, sort of tried to protect.

❧ The Peelers – a Very Different Kettle of Fish ... ❧

'The bloody, bloody peelers. You couldn't bribe them, you couldn't make friends with them – not like the old Bow Street Runners – and mostly the new boys were war veterans. If you had been in some of the wars lately and come back with all your bits still attached to your body, then that meant you was either a hard man or very, very lucky' – *Sharp Bob, a lawyer for criminals*

Sir Robert Peel (1788-1850)

The Big Peel was a cove who looked like a swell, but had the gleam of the street in his eye. Once he got his toe in the door of policing, suddenly there were policemen's boots everywhere, and life got a little tricky for those people on the edge of society.

A safe seat ...

Peel became an MP when he was only 21 – for a constituency in Ireland which only had 24 voters! He went on to become Home Secretary (once) and Prime Minister (twice). Whilst Home Secretary he changed policing in London for ever.

... and a special pig

Peel is credited with developing a specific breed of pig – the Tamworth.

DID YOU KNOW?

- Policemen were known as 'peelers' or 'bobbies' after Sir Robert Peel.

- They also got nicknamed 'PC Plod' since they had to walk a regular route at a slow pace.

- The first policeman ever was given the number 1 – and was sacked four hours later for being drunk on duty.

- The peelers wore long blue tailcoats and tall hats, which were reinforced at the crown with an iron ring – protection if anyone wanted to bash their head!

- They wore a stiff 'stock' around their neck to prevent garrotting.

- They carried a wooden truncheon, a rattle (later a whistle), a cutlass in a scabbard, and handcuffs.

- They wouldn't take no for an answer, and mostly they wouldn't take any answer at all from anyone unless it was: 'It's a fair cop, I'll come quietly, sir.'

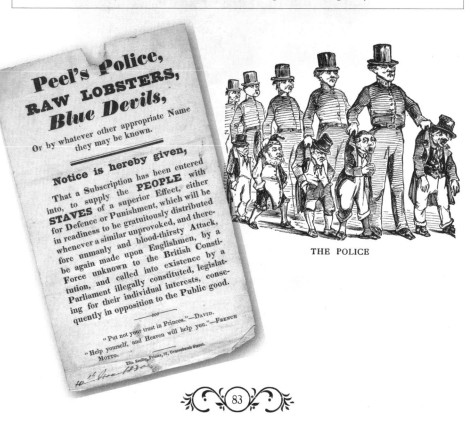

THE POLICE

·❧ If You Wanted to Forgo a Trip to Scotland Yard ... ❧·

It was easy to fall foul of the law. Just consider some of the petty crimes which might get a body into trouble:

(a) **THE FOLLOWING WILL** be summarily suppressed on appeal to the nearest police-constable:

Abusive language; Areas left open without sufficient fence.
Baiting animals; Betting in streets; Bonfires in streets; Books, obscene, selling in streets.
Carpet-beating; Cattle, careless driving of; Cock-fighting.
Dogs loose or mad; Doors, knocking at; Drunk and disorderly persons; Dust, removal of, between 10 a.m. and 7 p.m.
Exercising horses to annoyance of persons.
Firearms, discharging; Fireworks, throwing in streets; Furious driving.
Games, playing in streets.
Indecent exposure.
Lamps, extinguishing.
Mat-shaking after 8 a.m.
Obscene singing; Offensive matters, removal of, between 6 a.m. and 12 night.
Ringing door bells without excuse.
Slides, making in streets; Stone-throwing.

(b) **THE FOLLOWING WILL** require an application to the police-courts:

Cesspools, foul.
Dead body, infectious, retained in room where persons live.
Letting infected house or room.
Manure, non-removal of; Milk, exposing, unfit for consumption.
Trades, offensive (keeping pigs, soap-house, slaughter-house, or manufactures in trade causing effluvia, &c.).

– Extract from *Dickens's Dictionary of London* by Charles Dickens Jr. (1879)

A PLEASANT STREET GAME.

Old Gent. "CONFOUND THE BOYS AND THEIR TOPS! WHERE ARE THE POLICE?"

Advice to a would-be policeman's sweetheart

'Never hang your affections on a policeman's staff. The force is proverbially fickle . . .'
– *Punch* (Jul.–Dec. 1845)

Plain-clothed policemen! There ought to be a law against it; everybody said so – it was, well, it was unfair. After all, if you saw a peeler walking around, well, maybe you would think once or twice about dipping into someone's pocket or dipping into something that didn't really belong to anyone really, when you came to think about it, or just possibly knocking off something from a barrow when the owner wasn't looking. After all, seeing policemen around kept you honest, didn't it? If they were going to lurk around like ordinary people they were basically asking you to commit crimes, weren't they?

A DETECTIVE'S DIARY
APRIL 1863

APRIL 1. RECEIVED intelligence of an audacious burglary with violence at Walker's Green. Consulted INSPECTOR WATCHER. Hired a cab, and in company with SERGEANT DODGETT, had a pleasant drive to Walker's Green. Amusing fellow, DODGETT. Arrived and looked over the premises. Good sherry. MARY ANNE, the cook, much frightened. Comforted her officially. Housemaid just recovering from the effects of a blow from a life-preserver. Lady of the house had been very roughly handled. Asked our opinion. We informed her that we were certain that there had been a burglary with violence. She thanked us for the information. Received a couple of sovereigns. Drove back to town. Pleasant day. Saw the Inspector in the evening, informed him that DODGETT and myself were sure that an audacious burglary with violence had been committed at Walker's Green.

APRIL 2. Prosecuted our inquiries vigorously. Drove with SERGEANT DODGETT to Walker's Green. Observed something that had escaped our notice yesterday. Two large panels had been cut out of the front door, leaving an aperture of about three feet square. Measured it carefully with a piece of red tape. A man's head might have passed through it. Housemaid still suffering, but able to speak to DODGETT. Sharp fellow, DODGETT. The girl's arm is much swollen and the mistress's head still bound up. We are both of opinion that violence must have been used.

APRIL 3. Walker's Green. Good sherry and refreshments. Lady of the house said that one of the burglars had light hair and was about five feet eight inches. We are on the track. MARY ANNE, the cook, hoped I wouldn't get into danger. CHARLOTTE, the housemaid, looked hard at DODGETT. Returning to town we saw a man answering to the description. Arrested him. Measured his head with the red tape. Locked him up.

APRIL 4. Man examined. Said he hadn't done it. Asked him how it was he came to have light hair and be five feet eight? Was confused. Found out that he'd only just arrived from Birmingham where he had lived all his life. Cautioned and discharged him.

APRIL 5. Saw a man in the street, very tall and dark-haired. DODGETT said that was his cunning. Took him up. Asked him why he hadn't light hair, and why he wasn't five feet eight inches? He was dumb-founded. Turned out to be INSPECTOR WATCHER'S father-in-law. Apologized and discharged him.

APRIL 6. Got him at last. Highly complimented on our sagacity by everyone. Wrote to MARY ANNE saying how we were getting on. Man confessed to the burglary, and was locked up.

APRIL 7. Man who said he did it now says he didn't. Had too much to drink, very sorry. Reprimanded and discharged. Letter from MARY ANNE saying that her mistress would be out tomorrow, and we must come down as she and CHARLOTTE had made a discovery.

APRIL 8, 9, 10. Called every day at Walker's Green. See no reason to alter our opinion that an audacious burglary had been committed with violence. CHARLOTTE said she'd got something to tell DODGETT. Sly dog, DODGETT. MARY ANNE communicated her discovery to me. Nice girl - with considerable savings. Inspector requested us to report progress. Did so, and assured him that we had now no doubt as to the perpetration of a burglary, most audacious, with violence at Walker's Green. Arrested several people during the remainder the month. Measured all their heads with the red tape. Cautioned and discharged them.

MAY. On the 1st of this month CHARLOTTE will become MRS DODGETT. From information she received from me, MARY ANNE accepts my hand. Bother INSPECTOR WATCHER and the burglary with violence.

– PUNCH (1863)

PLACES TO AVOID

If you live in the rookeries, you needs to be on your toes all the time. For not a body wants to get collared by the aforesaid peelers, or go up before the beak – for that gentleman would be likely to take one look at a lad with the arse hanging out of his britches (especially if it turned out he was in somebody else's britches) and figure he was guilty afore he even heard the evidence. And before you could cry uncle you'd be heading for the last jig of your life. But they can't arrest you if they can't lay a hand on you, and I reckons that's the way to avoid all them places no soul wants to see the inside of. And there's more than one to stay well clear of . . .

Number One . . . The Courts

The first and foremost place to avoid was the Old Bailey – also known as the Sessions House, the Justice Hall, or just 'up before the beak' by everyone Dodger grew up with.

DID YOU KNOW?

- The Old Bailey got its name from the street it is on, which follows the original wall or 'bailey' of the City of London.
- Before gas lighting came into use in the 19th century, the accused had a mirror above his face so that those watching could see if he had a shifty expression or looked as innocent as the day he was born.
- A day at the trials was a jolly good day out for some of London's 'respectable' folk – and an 'orrible murder always drew the crowds.

Solomon must have lied to policemen all over Europe, and with God on his side, and would be very unlikely in the presence of a peeler to know if the sky was blue.

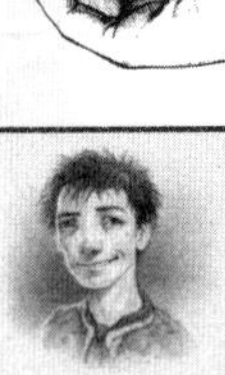

Trials were often very quick – the victim of the crime was able to stand up and make the accusation and the accused had to defend themselves. Often, it would just be the word of a policeman . . . who could be challenged by a barrister with oily words and an even oilier wig.

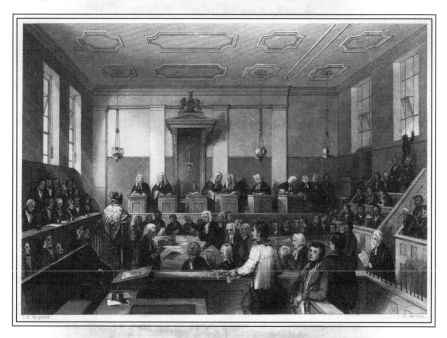

Social justice?

Victim or criminal? As a young thief might very well claim to the beak: 'It is all very fine for you to sit there, you that have not only had a jolly good breakfast, but can afford to sport a silver toothpick to pick your teeth with afterwards, it is all very fine for you to preach to me that I never shall do any good, but one of these days come to something that's precious bad, if I don't cut the ways of thieving, and take to honest ways . . . I ain't such a fool as not to know that it's better to walk in honest ways like them you've got into, and to wear gold chains and velvet waistcoats, than to prowl about in ragged corduroys, and dodge the pleeseman, and be a prig: but how am I to get into them sorts of honest ways? Will you give me a hist up to 'em? Will you give me a leg-up – I'm such a little cove, you see – on to the bottom round of the ladder that leads up to 'em?'

·⚜ Number Two ... The Prison House ⚜·

Wrongdoers could find themselves locked in gaol for the pettiest of crimes, for example this ten-year-old up before the beak at Wandsworth – young James Leadbeater.

CRIME:

Stealing celery to the value of one penny

SENTENCE:
Four days hard labour and a whipping

Other child criminals included ten-year-old George Davey, sentenced to one calendar month hard labour for stealing two live tame rabbits, and poor eleven-year-old Thomas Savage, who received ten strokes with a birch rod and four days hard labour for stealing some iron.

·⚜ Number Three ... Transportation ⚜·

In the early part of the century, transportation was very popular. Two for the price of one! Undesirable (or simply desperately poor) people shipped out of sight and out of mind, *and* it cost a lot less than prison. For simple thefts – often of food – even children under the age of ten could be sent thousands of miles away to lands on the other side of the world ... where who *knew* what might be in store for them.

I don't know very much about Australia, but Sol told me it's the other side of the world, so the way I see it that means that they must walk around upside down.

·❧ Number Four . . . Dancing the Hemp Fandango ❧·

'If there was a clink, then the clink was where you spent your days until they hanged you'

– Motto of a snakesman known to Dodger

DID YOU KNOW?

❀ Up until 1830 you could be hanged for stealing a horse or breaking into a house.

❀ Public hangings took place outside Newgate Gaol until 1868.

❀ By the time Victoria came to the throne, hanging was really only for traitors or murderers – like the Outlander assassin who Dodger brought to justice.

"PARTIES" FOR THE GALLOWS.

Newsvender.—" Now, MY MAN, WHAT IS IT ?"
Boy.—" I VONTS A NILLUSTRATED NEWSPAPER WITH A NORRID MURDER AND A LIKENESS IN IT."

Executions were considered a good day out for all the family – a very festive occasion with the odd riot thrown in for extra value. Jeer at the hangman! Buy a copy of the prisoner's dying speech! Cheer as the criminal kicked his last! Oh, and why not have a pickled whelk and a ginger beer to make a real day of it. And while you were eating that, why, a young dip might very well earn himself a pie or two by removing your pocketbook . . .

·❧ Number Five ... Bedlam Hospital ❧·

Fancied a different sort of day out? At one time, Bethlem Hospital – Europe's oldest hospital for the care and control of the insane – was a popular, nay essential, sight for any visitor to the metropolis. Fees were charged and the antics of the wretches within the unhappy mansion were considered a moral example of what could happen if anyone allowed their passions to rule their actions. Many patients were naked, or just covered with a single blanket, and chains and manacles were in common usage. You *really* wanted to know you could go home again when you'd had enough . . .

Dodger about Sweeney Todd: 'The poor devil was indeed more a candidate for Bedlam rather than the gallows, though any man with any sense but no money would choose the hangman any day.'

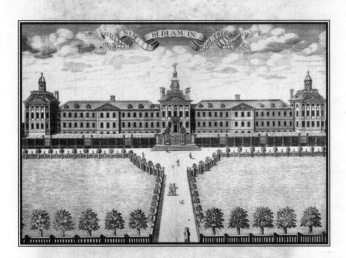

They're coming to take you away. . . !

A patient in a Victorian asylum? Here are some of the treatments that might have been in store for you:

❋ Bloodletting – by removing blood, the body would supposedly be more balanced. Unless too much was taken, in which case most bodies would become very *un*balanced and simply fall over.

* Hypnotism – for those suffering from 'hysteria' (often caused by an overactive womb, apparently, though Dodger himself had never heard of anyone's womb leaping into action or going to war).
* Induced vomiting.
* Solitary confinement.
* Leeches.
* Strait-jackets.
* Chains or manacles e.g. being chained to the bed at night.

And, of course, there was the Rotary Chair (see *Induced vomiting* above). The unfortunate patient would be strapped in, and the chair hoisted into the air and then spun round and round. The patient would become so disorientated that they would repent of their wickedness and alight a New Person. They usually repented of their last meal, all right . . .

A low-slung brow? Murderer! Big nose? Pickpocket!

A new-fangled science involved checking out the shape of someone's head and reading the lumps and bumps (assuming none had just been added by a blunt instrument, of course) to establish a person's temperament. Death-masks were made of prisoners' heads after hanging so that the eager young phrenologists could discover the typical look of someone likely to become a hardened criminal.

Howling at the moon?

The words 'lunatic' and 'lunacy' come from the Latin word for moon – *luna* – and mental patients have been shown to become more disturbed at the time of a full moon (though despite tales in the penny dreadfuls, no one of Dodger's acquaintance was ever seen to turn into a wolf on such a night). In the rookeries, though, a wolf would have been easy prey – and possibly a good dinner or two – for some of the night people . . .

WORK HARD, PLAY HARD

Walk across the bridges of London and take a look at all the entertainments: hordes of street people earning their daily crust by helping others forget the troubles they've had in earning their crust. For it's not only the nobby folk in their coach-and-fours who want to head out after dark for a bit of fun and amusement; a body who's spent a day doing hard labour in return for enough pennies to pay for a bed for the night and a pie to eat is also going to want to have some fun. And where there's a want, there's always going to be someone to come up with the goods. And it should go without saying that young ladies going out by themselves in the big city must keep their hand on their ha'penny – I mean, the local girls learns how things are on the streets, but the blossoms from faraway and exotic places like Uxbridge and Gerrards Cross are easy meat to the smart telling gentlemen who are jingling their pockets. And who knows what it might be that they was a-jingling.

·❧ Penny Gaffs ☙·

LADIES AND GENTLEMEN TO THE FRONT PLACES MUST PAY TWOPENCE

Small theatres known as 'penny gaffs' – the standard entrance fee being a penny – were everywhere in the East End of Victorian London. The front of a shop would be removed (yes, with the owner's knowledge), the entrance decorated, and comic singers would exhort passersby to part with their pennies and come on in. Inside, along with a band perched on a table or two, the entertainment was noisy, boisterous and often very naughty. All good value for a penny! Outside, and for no extra charge, there was the added enjoyment of watching a policeman trying to keep order.

Any flash dancing? 'Yes! Lots! Show their legs an' all, prime!'

Flash songs, sailors' songs or patriotic songs were much enjoyed – as were some dramas, mostly tragedies though, without too many jaw-breakers (long words). Best were those that told the tales of famous highwaymen (like Dick Turpin) or stories of robbers and murderers hanged at Newgate – and if the actors ran out of time, well, they would just race through the final bit before chucking everyone out.

A favourite song of the day amongst the donkey-loving costermongers was called 'Duck-Legged Dick':

'Duck-legged Dick had a donkey,
And his lush loved much to swill,
One day he got rather lumpy,
And got sent seven days to the mill.
His donkey was taken to the green-yard,
A fate which he never deserved.

Oh! It was such a regular mean yard,
That alas! The poor moke got starved.
Oh! Bad luck can't be prevented,
Fortune she smiles or she frowns,
He's best off that's contented,
To mix, sirs, the ups and the downs.'

A theme with similar sentiments to Kipling's soon-to-be-written 'If'.

Skirt dancing

A popular pastime for the nobs was to watch skirt dancing, where women would artfully swish and swirl up to 12 metres of fabric. (Dodger himself liked a bit of skirt, but all the prancing about wasn't really his cup of tea.)

DID YOU KNOW?

In 1884, Joseph Merrick, known as the Elephant Man because of his severe deformities, was exhibited as a freak in a penny gaff in Whitechapel.

–⁕ Treading the Boards ⁕–

Dodger knew that actors didn't get paid very much – he always reckoned that the only reason to be on a stage would be to rob it. But for a really good night out, the music hall was the place to go.

Here, for just a few pennies, a whole host of different acts did their 'turns' – with the emphasis on good comic songs and the audience frequently joining in with boos, cheers, burps and belches.

'Lions comiques' were especially popular – entertainers who parodied nobby toffs and sang songs about booze, ladies and laziness. They would typically wear furs and diamonds, and lampoon the hedonism of the upper classes.

> 'A man appears on the platform, dressed in outlandish clothes, and ornamented with whiskers of ferocious length and hideous hue, and proceeds to sing verse after verse of pointless twaddle, interspersed with a blatant "chorus", in which the audience is requested to join' – *The Tomahawk* (September 1867)

One famous London music hall was Wilton's – built in the 1850s in the East End, near the docks.

THE MIDDLESEX THEATRE
••••••• OF DRURY LANE ••••••

"THE GREATEST SIXPENCE EVER SPENT!"

MONDAY, 14TH SEPTEMBER AND DURING THE WEEK

By particular desire expressed to us by our audience, and under the patronage of LEWIS G. MORGAN we are pleased to inform you that this week we

PRESENT

a comic turn, by

GEORGE LEYBOURNE

Dwell upon the hardships of wealth and influence and learn to take pity upon those thusly disposed as GEORGE LEYBOURNE
introduces
'CHAMPAGNE CHARLIE'

EXCEPT WEDNESDAY WHEN, AS ALWAYS, THERE WILL BE A GRAND MORNING PERFORMANCE OF THE PANTOMIME

Messers Thomas Bliss, Martin Morris and Jacob Corn perform

A PECULIAR POSITION!

the fashionable COMEDY with many meanings!

BETTER THE DEVIL YOU KNOW

A tale of fidelity and honour in the marital arena, performed for us by the players of the Colchester Rep. Theatre, on tour this season.

A COMIC SONG, By Mr. H Fistral
A SCOTCH DANCE, By Mr. Pardleton and wife
&
SECRETS WORTH KNOWING
as performed by Mr. M Rindel

our evening concludes with the National Anthem and a perfomance by those great favourites

THE BLUE RIBBON GIRLS

The SALOONS under the Management of Messrs. Dines & Co.
Doors to open at Seven o' clock for commencement at Eight

WILTON'S NEW MUSIC HALL, WELLCLOSE SQUARE

DID YOU KNOW?

- Up to a thousand people would squeeze in to watch a show – although it was supposed to only have room for 300!

- Unlike theatres for the nobs, people could eat, drink and smoke whilst watching the entertainment.

- Other famous music halls included the Canterbury Music Hall in Lambeth, the Middlesex in Drury Lane – which was known as the Old Mo – and variety theatres like the Egyptian Hall in Piccadilly.

Some of the stars of the music hall . . .

Champagne Charlie . . .

George Leybourne (1842–84) was a famous 'lion comique', always immaculately dressed as a nobby young swell. His songs included 'Champagne Charlie' and 'The Daring Young Man on the Flying Trapeze'. And he was so popular that he was employed at the Canterbury Music Hall in 1868 on a contract paying him £25 a week plus a carriage drawn by four white horses.

LOUNGING IN THE AQ.

T. L. CLAY.
GEORGE LEYBOURNE

Great Little Leno . . .

Dan Leno (1860–1904) was first on the stage at the age of nine, when he became famous for his clog-dancing. His comic patter made him a popular performer.

The Queen of the Music Hall . . .

Marie Lloyd (1870–1922) turned professional at the age of 14. Her songs were considered too saucy for the bigger theatres.

. . . And some of the variety on offer!

Including good gawps at anyone with a physical curiosity – something Dodger didn't himself like to do. Those on show, however, often made a jolly good living (up to £20 a week by the end of the century) out of exhibiting themselves.

·⚜ The Arts ⚜·——

'You must raise your play, Mister Dodger, because no man should waste his life tramping through sewers when he could be sailing through literature and the theatre' – *Angela Burdett-Coutts to Dodger*

Introduced to the theatre by Angela Burdett-Coutts (officially, anyway, since his snakesman days had led him in and out of several theatres before this happy expedition), Dodger found himself seated in a box watching a bunch of coves in bed sheets spouting a lot of words written by a geezer called William Shakespeare – *Julius Caesar*. He figured that the play was very much like a fight on the streets, except that for some reason they used words a lot more than their weapons.

DID YOU KNOW?

 Pantomimes could last up to five hours.

 320 Regent Street was formerly the site of the Theatrical Dental Institution, where actors and members of the music hall profession could go to obtain the 'Very Best Artificial Teeth at Greatly Reduced Fees and Easy Payments'.

ROYAL

OLYMPUS 🏛 THEATRE

WYKE STREET, STRAND

LESSEES AND MANAGERS, MESSER,S

H. BLOEMEN and T. SOPER

IMPLORE YOU TO CONSIDER

AN EVENING AT THE OLYMPUS

DOORS OPEN AT SEVEN FOR AN EIGHT O' CLOCK PERFORMANCE

IN THE COMPANY OF FRIENDS AND FAMILY

FOR

WILLIAM SHAKESPEARE'S

THEATRICAL MASTERPIECE

JULIUS CAESAR

PERFORMED BY

Marcus Winerts	**BRUTUS**
James Nisbeck	*JULIUS CAESAR*
Christopher Lewis	ANTHONY
Philip King	CASSIUS
Justin Thompson	OCTAVIUS
Peter Smith	CASCA

PERFORMANCES NIGHTLY

MATINEES WEDNS. THURS.

THROUGHOUT JULY

EXCEPT THE FIRST AND THIRD SUNDAYS OF THE MONTH

FIRST PRICE :---- Stalls, 5s.   Upper Box Stalls 4s
    Dress Circle, 4s.   Pit, 2s.   Gallery 1s.

SECOND PRICE :---- Upper Box Stalls, 2s.
    Dress Circle, 2s.   Pit, 1s.   Gallery 6d.

PRIVATE BOXES, £2 2s & £1 1s. FAMILY BOXES, £3 3s.

THE BOX-OFFICE OPEN, DAILY, FROM 11 till 5 O'Clock
Under the direction of Mr. S. Stapleton

PLACES RETAINABLE THE WHOLE EVENING, MAY BE TAKEN AT
THE BOX-OFFICE, WHERE THE PAYMENT OF ONE SHILLING
WILL SECURE FROM ONE TO EIGHT SEATS.

CHILDREN UNDER THE AGE OF THREE YEARS
OF AGE CANNOT, ON ANY ACCOUNT, BE ADMITTED

·❧ Street Performers ☙·

For those with less specie to splash, the streets were full of entertainment, one of Dodger's favourites being the Happy Families wagon: a cart which bore a cage in which a little menagerie of animals all lived together in peace, despite more usually eating each other. There would be:

- ✴ a baboon
- ✴ a dog
- ✴ a cat
- ✴ a mouse
- ✴ a couple of birds
- ✴ a snake.

Miss Simplicity: 'Why on earth doesn't the cat eat the mouse, Dodger?'

Dodger: 'Well, I think the old man is not one to tell you his secrets, but some people say if they are brought up together with some kindness, they become just that, a happy family. Although I have been told that should a mouse who has not yet been introduced to the snake come in through the bars, it would become the snake's dinner very quickly.'

According to one description, this was not all. The reader may suspect that this observer had spent some time in the public house and imbibed a considerable amount before furnishing his account . . .

'The performance would commence by opening the cage door and calling the cats by popular pugilistic names. They came, were invested with boxing-gloves, stood on their hind legs and pretended to spar. After a time the man would ask the dog "if he didn't see the family fighting?" He would bark a reply, and, charging out of the cage, interpose, growling, between the combatants, sometimes upsetting them far from gently. Having stopped the fight he retired wagging his tail. But the cats, encouraged by their master, set to again and were once more stopped. When this palled a little by repetition a medal was hung round the neck of one cat and a bandage tied round one eye of the other, and they were told to sit at two corners of the platform.

Then, under their noses almost, the mice walked a tight rope carrying balancing-poles, *à la mode de Blondin*. A bird fired a toy cannon, and another, affecting to be killed, permitted itself to be placed in a coffin and towed away on a hearse without a sign of life till the carriage stopped at the cage door, when it revived and hopped in. The supposed murderer was executed by placing his head in a running noose, suspended from a gibbet, which another bird tightened by pulling. Then the showman, after going round with the cap, sought another pitch. The public always provided a crowd, although there was a notion abroad that such effects could only be produced by ill-treatment. Whether the Police deemed these displays obstructive or the Society for the Prevention of Cruelty to Animals interfered I don't know, but Happy Families grew scarcer and scarcer. The last I saw was on the Thames Embankment by Charing Cross Bridge some time in the 1880s.'
– Extract from *London and Londoners in the Eighteen-Fifties and Sixties* by Alfred Rosling Bennett (1920)

A fool and his money are soon parted . . .

For those who felt Lady Luck crouching on their shoulder, the street was the place where entertainment *and* profit could be achieved – though Dodger himself had never seen *anyone* guess correctly when the cheery man asked you to bet on which thimble he had placed a pea under. Sooner or later, *surely* it would be under the one you picked – but probably not even God could have followed those nimble fingers . . .

Clowns in horse-hair wigs or striding high on stilts, salamanders (fire-eaters), 'equilibrists' (balancers), dancing bears, tame camels, sword-swallowers, contortionists writhing at your feet (a very adventurous profession, given what else might be at your feet) and shows of pig-faced ladies, industrious fleas, giants and spotted boys . . . all life and more could be seen for a fee on the London streets. Though all life might have wished for slightly better jokes . . .

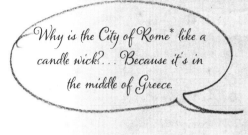

Why is the City of Rome* like a candle wick? . . . Because it's in the middle of Greece.

A horse has ten legs: he has two forelegs and two hind ones. Two fores are eight, and two others are ten!

DID YOU KNOW?
Amidst the crowds, varied singers and bands competed for pennies – and the overwhelming noise was such that sometimes people simply paid them to go away!

Organ – and teeth – grinding
London was home to over a thousand organ grinders in the 1860s, much to the dismay of Dodger's friends and associates. When scientist Charles Babbage, an outspoken opponent of these 'instruments of torture', died in 1871, his obituary said that he lived almost 80 years in spite of 'organ-grinding persecutors'.

Handy with your fists?
Able to give someone a 'noser'? In the public houses, landlords would hire out gloves (about tuppence a night) and two lads would give the crowd a real spectacle of a fight – 'Not for money but for beer and "a lark",' though the best could go on to be professionals. The winner was the first to give the other a smack on the nose – and blood was usually demanded to prove the blow had landed. Dodger knew several people he'd be happy to give a noser to, and he didn't need no money neither to do so!

* He would have it Rome.

People thought that a ragged face was a sign of a professional boxer, but it wasn't – it was a sign of an amateur boxer. Good boxers liked to be pretty; it put the contenders off their guard.

DID YOU KNOW?

James Kelly and Jonathan Smith set the record for the longest ever bare-knuckle fight in 1855 – 17 rounds over 6 hours and 15 minutes. They were fighting in Australia (and probably not upside down, as Dodger once believed). Kelly won.

PLEASING PROPOSAL.

"WE HAVE HEARD, CONFIDENTIALLY, AS HOW YOU'RE THE GENT AS COMED OVER THE WATER ALONG WITH HEENAN; AND MY YOUNG FRIEND, THE ENTHUSIASTIC POT-BOY, WANTS TO PUT THE GLOVES ON WITH YER."

And after watching the fight in the pub, spectators often had the jolly chance to participate in a fight of their own *outside* the establishment . . .

Punch and Judy

'That's the way to do it!'

In the streets, where people had been squashed down so low that fists were a common currency, everyone still laughed at the antics of Mister Punch and the motley crew of characters telling his story. And anyone who got a regular punch would cheer when the murdering Mister Punch got his comeuppance and headed for the prison house at the end of Act One.

A typical Punch and Judy show featured Punch, Judy, the Child, the Beadle, Scaramouche, Nobody, Jack Ketch, the Grand Senor, the Doctor, the Devil, Toby the Dog, Merry Andrew and the Blind Man – but a showman could get away with just four characters (including Punch himself, of course).

DID YOU KNOW?

❋ The character of Mr Punch is descended from Pulcinella, a clown who appeared in travelling theatres in Italy in the 15th century.

❋ Showmen used a *swazzle* – a kind of whistle about the size of a knee-buckle tied up with black cotton – to get the squawking voice of Punch. It could take someone up to six months to learn how to use it properly.

❋ Punch would normally be dressed in a jester's outfit with a tasselled hat. To make him look like a real villain, he was usually hunchbacked with a big hooked nose, a pointy chin and a nasty stick he used to wallop other characters.

❋ Scaramouche was a character who first appeared in Italian theatre; a clown in a black mask who was a bit of a rogue. In some Punch and Judy shows, Punch knocked Scaramouche's head off, and as a result 'scaramouche' became a common term for puppets with necks that can be extended.

❋ A 'bottler' would be used to draw in the audience and collect their pennies in a bottle. He might also have to help with sound effects or play music.

PUNCH & JUDY

LADIES AND GENTLEMEN
AND **CHILDREN**
FOR YOUR ENTERTAINMENT
MISTER PUNCH AND MISTRESS JUDY!
SEE PUNCH DROP THE BABY!
SEE JUDY WALLOP PUNCH!
CAN THE DOCTOR AVOID BEING WALLOPED?
WILL PUNCH ESCAPE THE NOOSE?
SHOW COMMENCES AT
2.30 P.M. PROMPT
1ᵈ ONE PENNY **1**ᵈ
A CHILD

❄ 'Happaratus' like a set of gallows, a ladder, a horse, a bell and a stuffed dog were usually used. Sometimes a smart little dog would play Toby, rather than it being a stuffed toy. Dodger once offered Solomon's dog, Onan, up for the job but Onan would have cleared the crowd, not added to it.

❄ The best earnings were had by performing in front of gents' houses – performing in the open street could bring in as little as threepence.

OFFICIAL CENSORSHIP OF PANTOMIME.

Policeman. "I WOULDN'T HAVE MINDED A QUIET PERFORMANCE; BUT TO BEGIN INSULTIN' THE LAWR UNDER MY WERY EYES!—(*Waxing wroth*)— MOVE ON! OR BLOW'D IF I DON'T RUN YER IN!"

'In my opinion the street Punch is one of those extravagant reliefs from the realities of life which would lose its hold upon the people if it were made moral and instructive. I regard it as quite harmless in its influence, and as an outrageous joke which no one in existence would think of regarding as an incentive to any kind of action or as a model for any kind of conduct. It is possible, I think, that one secret source of pleasure very generally derived from this performance . . . is the satisfaction the spectator feels in the circumstance that likenesses of men and women can be so knocked about, without any pain or suffering.'
– Extract from *The Letters of Charles Dickens*, vol. V (1847–9)

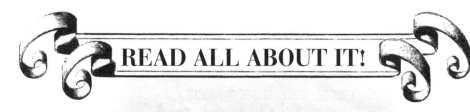

READ ALL ABOUT IT!

Whatever Sol said to me about needing to broaden my horizons, I'd always figured that a newspaper was really only something handy to use in the jakes, but my friend Mister Charlie then showed me how the press can actually change the world with a little scribble or two. A lad can become a hero, a politician can become a champion – and all because of a few careful words writ down and then read by many. You must have 'eard of Charlie? Never seen such a man for scribble, scribble, scribble. He wanted to be a peeler, a defective . . .

In which we meet those who specialize in the Most Heinous and Extravagant Usage of the English Vocabulary in Their Extraordinary Efforts to Report on Recent Events and Activities in Order to Acquire for Themselves the Highest Pecuniary Remunerations.

DID YOU KNOW?

Journalists used to be known as 'penny-liners' as they were paid a penny a line, so they tried not to use one word if a whole library would do.

·❧ Fleet Street ❧·

Fleet Street was the heart of London's news – a place where everywhere you looked there were ink-stained men and boys running from place to place (in an emergency, *even on the spot*) to make sure that the population of the great metropolis could read about:

- ❋ *what* had happened – an 'orrible murder was the favourite
- ❋ *why* it had happened
- ❋ *what* would happen next – Newgate or the Tyburn jig?
- ❋ and – most importantly, so that readers could plan a day out if a hanging was involved – *when* it would happen.

Hard Times for a river?

Fleet Street was named after the river Fleet – a river that had fallen on Hard Times, being more akin to an open sewer with Great Expectations. It bore not just water but a regular tribute of dead cats and other detritus down to good ol' Father Thames.

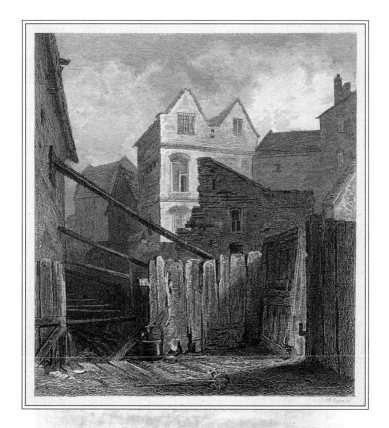

·❧ The *Morning Chronicle* ❧·

The Wisdom of Solomon: 'Onto the world that is, people paint the world that they would like. Therefore they *like* to see dragons slain, and where there are gaps, public imagination will fill the void.'

Dodger was introduced to the world of the Press when Mister Charlie Dickens arranged to meet him at his offices at the *Morning Chronicle* – Dickens's first employer, which also published Mister Mayhew's articles on the London poor. Although Dodger never became a proper friend of the newspapers – the principle that you never got your name writ down anywhere if you could avoid it was nailed to his backbone – it was hard not to feel even a little bit accommodating towards people who wanted to call him a hero and raise a reward for him based only on a bit of misunderstanding.

Mister Charlie Dickens (1812–70)

'They say he can take one look at you and he's got a perfect study of you, from the way you talk down to the way you pick your nose' – *Solomon about Charlie*

DID YOU KNOW?

❈ Dickens's father was thrown into prison for debt and the young Charles had to leave school to work in a factory making pots of boot-blacking. He earned six shillings a week for pasting labels onto pots.

❈ He wanted to be an actor, but missed his chance to audition when he caught a cold at the wrong time.

❈ He wrote short stories in the *Chronicle* under the name 'Boz'.

❈ His first novel, *The Posthumous Papers of the Pickwick Club* (also known as *The Pickwick Papers*), was originally published as a series of shilling instalments.

❈ He used his own experiences – and the names of people he had met – in many of his novels. For instance, the boy who showed him how to paste the labels on pots in the factory had the name 'Fagin'.

❈ With Angela Burdett-Coutts, Dickens helped to found 'Urania Cottage' – a home for women who had 'fallen' but who wanted to get up again (mostly by getting married or going to a new country).

'I sometimes suspect he would love to be a peeler if I let him; he'd make a good copper if he didn't scribble, scribble, scribble all the time, I am sure' – *Sir Robert Peel to Dodger, about Charlie*

·❦ *Punch* and Tenniel ❦·

That's the way to make 'em laugh . . . and think!

Founded in 1841 by Dodger's friend Mister Henry Mayhew and engraver Ebenezer Landells, with an initial investment of just £25, *Punch* became a weekly paper known for its humour and social comment. And all for just threepence!

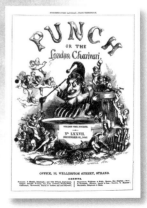

John Tenniel (1820–1914)

Another scribbler – but of a different kind. Tenniel was an artist who produced splendid cartoons, often with serious political punch, for *Punch* itself.

- ❀ Tenniel drew an astonishing 2,165 cartoons for *Punch*.
- ❀ He also drew the pictures for Lewis Carroll's *Alice's Adventures in Wonderland*, and *Through the Looking-Glass*.
- ❀ Queen Victoria knighted him in 1893 and he was known as a living national treasure, managing to enjoy this moniker for 21 years before he became a dead national treasure in 1914.

A dodgy eye?

It's even more astonishing that Tenniel could draw so well, since as a young man he was injured in the right eye by his father's sword when they were fencing. Over the years, he lost the sight in this eye . . . a bit of a disadvantage for an artist.

Model needed! A Tenniel cartoon that showed his daily dilemmas . . .

A FRIEND IN NEED.

Our Artist. "OH! MY DEAR OLD BOY! I'M SO GLAD TO SEE YOU! MY MODEL HASN'T COME, AND I'M IN A REGULAR FIX; SO, P'RAPS YOU WOULDN'T MIND BEING MY DEAD ARTILLERYMAN FOR AN HOUR OR SO."

·❧ Penny Dreadfuls ❧·——

A penny dreadful, penny awful, penny 'orrible or penny blood . . .

There wasn't a lot of reading in the rookeries. Who had the time when there was a living to be made? But lurid serials were published every week, and costing only one penny a piece they were very popular amongst young readers – the more lurid the better.

- Hold your breath as highwayman Dick Turpin – a scallywag of the first order – cheats the hangman as he sets off on his extraordinary ride to York on Black Bess (the whole story took 254 episodes to tell – that's nearly five years at one penny dreadful a week!).
- Thrill to the tale of Spring-Heeled Jack as he bounds over tall buildings, claws at the ready, his red eyes gleaming in the shadows!
- Shiver at the blood-soaked antics of Varney the Vampire, and cheer as he meets his terrible doom by throwing himself into the pits of hell within the volcano Vesuvius!

Many would buy just the first in a serial to see what it was like – and others simply went for the largest so that 'when they've got the reading out of it, it's worth a halfpenny for the barrow'. Or, of course, it might come in useful in the privy . . . where you could have the satisfaction of wiping your arse on the most dastardly villains.

But one of the most popular penny dreadfuls told the terrible tale of the Demon Barber of Fleet Street . . .

—·❧ A Close Shave? ❧·—

The penny dreadful telling the tale of Mister Sweeney Todd and his razor* was a huge success – but Dodger, who was friendly with a number of old sweats and knew that Sweeney Todd was described as having been a barber-surgeon on the battlefields of Europe, felt that Mister Todd was most likely as much a victim as the six men whose throats he had cut (though nobody asked them what their views were, and they most probably would have disagreed). For war leaves men not just minus limbs, but often minus bits of their minds . . .

Mister Todd killed, but he wasn't a killer. Maybe if he'd never had to go to that blessed war, he wouldn't have gone right off his head.

*Sweeney Todd was a fictional character and was used in Terry Pratchett's *Dodger* for dramatic effect, but unlike other personages in this guide, he was only a creation of an imaginative mind. But that is not to say that the wartime experiences of many might easily led to similar actions.

THE ILLUSTRATED
POLICE NEWS

A WEEKLY RECORD OF CRIME AND MALEFICENCE.

N° 235 — SATURDAY, NOVEMBER 13, 1845 — [PRICE ONE PENNY.]

MURDER MOST FOUL IN FLEET STREET

In a cellar awash with the blood of Innocent Victims a renowned reporter, Mr Charles Dickens, witnessed the arrest of Mr Sweeney Todd, a deranged killer whose terrible deeds will go down in history as one of the most horrible crimes our capital city has ever seen.

Innocent customers of this fiend's establishment were lured by the sign 'Easy shaving for a penny, as good as you will find anywhere,' and once in his chair of death, with manic strength he slit their throats to the bone.

His reign of terror was brought to an end only by the courage and agility of a young hero, who Police Officers tell was

WITH RAZOR AND KNIFE HE DISPATCHED HIS VICTIMS.

seen to face down the killer, even as Mister Todd brandished his dreadful razor towards the lad's unprotected throat. The young hero stepped fearlessly forward, wrestled the villain to the floor and removed that weapon from the Demon Barber's cursed hand.

And to his great credit, despite having so nearly lost his own life, the modest lad pleaded that society should now take pity on this wretched man, a victim of the recent wars – earnestly and most eloquently begging me and you, dear reader, to appreciate that: 'He wasn't a demon, mister, although I reckon he may have seen Hell, and I ain't a hero, sir, I really ain't. He wasn't bad, he was mad, and sad, and lost in his 'ead.'

The *News Chronicle*, for whom Mr Charles Dickens reports, is proposing to raise a subscription for this young hero of the lower orders in recognition of his valour and moral fortitude in rising above his lowly station.

FROM PIP TO JACK
VIA A BIT OF DODGING . . .

As I knows very well, the name a body is given can bring a lot of trouble – picking up the moniker 'Dodger' in the orphanage where I grew up was one of the best things I ever did. I definitely wanted to lose the name they gave me when I was left there as a baby (Pip Stick). Names might not maketh the man, but they certainly go a long way to making a child's life a misery if you get yourself saddled with a wrong 'un!

Many things influenced what a child might be called, and nobby names – often sucking up to royalty with a lot of young Georges and Victorias – tended to be different from names given in the rookeries. With a bit of wishful thinking that a child might personify their name, many Victorian families would opt for virtues like Charity, Hope or Mercy – Jane Mayhew chose 'Simplicity', for instance.

DID YOU KNOW?

 Queen Victoria and Prince Albert had nine children – Victoria Adelaide Mary, Albert Edward, Alice Maud Mary, Alfred Ernest Albert, Helena Augusta Victoria, Louise Caroline Alberta, Arthur William Patrick, Leopold George Duncan and Beatrice Mary Victoria. So a lot of names to copy there, then!

 The ten most popular Victorian names for boys, however, were: John, William, James, George, Charles, Joseph, Frank, Robert, Edward and Henry. A lot of old kings listed there but not an Albert amongst them.

 And for girls: Mary, Anna, Margaret, Helen, Elizabeth, Ruth, Florence, Ethel, Emma and Marie.

But most of Dodger's acquaintances – those living in the rookeries – had names they had picked up along the way, like himself. Hence he knew people by handles such as Dirty Benjamin, One-Armed Dave or Messy Bessie, not forgetting old sweats like poor old Stumpy Higgins.

But of course, in the rookeries, the best names were those that no one could remember when a body turned up asking questions: 'Dodger? Never 'eard of him, guv.' Or, 'Mister Dodger? Never clapped eyes on 'im, guv'nor! You must be thinking of some other cove.'

——— ❧ London Street Names ❧ ———

The East End of London was full of names that related to the working man's occupation – streets like Ironmonger Lane, or Three Cranes Lane (where three strong timber cranes stood on the wharf) – or were based on local churches or important personages who had lived there. But some of the names are harder to fathom . . .

Battle Bridge Lane – a very old name, marking the site of the battle where the Romans beat Boadicea.

Cheapside – based on an old word for a market, 'chepe'.

Crutched Friars – where there used to be a house of Crouched, or Crossed, Friars, founded in the 13th century.

Fetter Lane – 'fewterers' was a term for a bunch of idle layabouts who hung around this area.

Fyfoot Lane – just five foot wide at one end!

Mayfair – the site of an old fair, St James's Fair, held every May.

Pall Mall – a medieval game known as Pell-Mell (a bit like croquet) was played here in the time of Charles I.

Poultry – a great place to buy a chicken! A little courtyard off it was called Scalding Alley, where the dead fowl were plucked and scalded.

Seven Dials – seven streets and a seven-faced sundial on a column. Mr Catnach, a printer of ballads, lived here – for a penny, you could buy a yard of ballads!

Shadwell – named after a fine spring (a 'shady well') near the church.

Smithfield – this name most likely came from the number of blacksmiths who used to set up their forges here when there was a big horse and cattle market in the area.

Tokenhouse Yard – the site of the old Mint-house, where tokens were issued and exchanged.

Wapping – an old name for a ship's rope was a 'wapp' and there were always lots of seagoing trades in the Wapping area – people making sails, ropes and ships.

LANDMARKS FOR THE ENQUIRING YOUNG MIND

Many a body never ventures beyond the square mile or so that makes up the streets I grew up in. But outside that . . . well, if you start to look a bit further, there is another London – a glittering, shiny, sparkly new world with a new young queen and the need for new people. Solomon opened my eyes to the opportunities out there and Miss Simplicity gave me a reason to up my game.

Dodger was right. Real prospects beckoned for a Smart Young Man. And the Victorian Age wasn't happy with just a glorious city, oh no, they wanted a glorious city with knobs on. But we begin, as ever, with the patch that Dodger knew so well – the area known as the East End, where most of the hurrying, scurrying crowd just minded their own business, though with plenty also keeping an eye out for the happy opportunity of minding someone else's business – or belongings – too.

The Bow Bells

Tradition says that to be a true Cockney, a child has to be born within the sound of the Bow bells. Nobody says if the bells should be ringing at the time, though, nor whether the mother would be likely to be listening out for a happy peal, rather than a happy gurgle.

DID YOU KNOW?

 The Bow bells aren't in Bow; they are the bells of the church of St Mary-le-Bow in Cheapside, right in the heart of the Square Mile. Apparently the bells can be heard six miles to the east, five miles to the north, three miles to the south and four miles to the west (though in Dodger's day it may have depended on how much screaming was going on in the streets at the time).

Milestones on some roads from London showed the mileage from the church door of St Mary-le-Bow, and a cast-iron bow and bells were marked on the mileposts.

Oranges and Lemons

The Bow bells featured in this popular children's singing game. Two players create an arch, which other children have to pass through before helping to make an even bigger arch. When the last line of the song is reached, the unfortunate child passing through the tunnel of arms must sprint to avoid getting caught by the others. But the rhyme also provides a great list of some of the bells of London.

'Oranges and lemons,
Say the bells of St Clement's.

You owe me five farthings,
Say the bells of St Martin's.

When will you pay me?
Say the bells of Old Bailey.

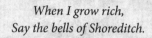

When I grow rich,
Say the bells of Shoreditch.

When will that be?
Say the bells of Stepney.

I do not know,
Says the great bell of Bow.

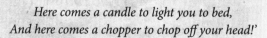

Here comes a candle to light you to bed,
And here comes a chopper to chop off your head!'

DID YOU KNOW?

The final lines of the verse refer to the condemned cells when villains were executed at Tyburn Tree. At midnight on the Sunday before their fate they'd be told of their execution date by candlelight by the bellman of the church of St Sepulchre, and the night before, a large hand bell known as the Execution Bell would be rung.

And an Even Bigger Bell . . .

The big daddy of all the bells in London has to be . . . the huge bell at Westminster, 200 feet up the tower: Big Ben.

DID YOU KNOW?

✳ Sixteen horses were needed to pull the huge bell to the tower on trolleys.

✳ The bell cracked while it was being tested and a second bell had to be made at Whitechapel Bell Foundry. This one lasted two months before cracking!

✳ Third time lucky . . . the bell was repaired and the hammer reset to hit it in a different place.

✳ The bell is 7 feet 6 inches tall and 9 feet in diameter.

London Bridge

It somehow seemed to Dodger that the city and the river were the same creature, but some parts were just wetter than others. One of the busiest thoroughfares in London – and one of the only ways to cross the river if you didn't want to take a waterman – London Bridge also spawned a children's game that was almost identical to *Oranges and Lemons* (clearly the young players liked to pretend to chop heads off), whilst another version gave a nod to the throngs of pickpockets you might encounter if you were so unwise as to cross the bridge without keeping a tight grip on your pocketbook.

'London Bridge is falling down,
Falling down, falling down.
London Bridge is falling down,
My fair lady.'

Or:

'Who has stole my watch and chain,
Watch and chain, watch and chain;
Who has stole my watch and chain,
My fair lady?

Off to prison you must go,
You must go, you must go;
Off to prison you must go,
My fair lady.'

·❧ Piccadilly Circus ❧·

The centre of London – and where all of London seemed to want to arrive in a growler . . .

'Piccadilly Circus, guv, all fouled up 'cos of the rain . . . people are cutting in like Christmas dinner. I don't know why they're always messing about with the roads, but I reckon it's the four-horsers that are causing this lot – they shouldn't be allowed in the city!'
– growler driver to Dodger

✻ It is believed that Piccadilly Circus got its name from a tailor in the 16th century who sold 'pickadels' – a ruffed collar for men – from his shop there.

✻ Some of the people who have lived in Piccadilly include Lord Byron, Lord Palmerston and Nelson's mistress Lady Hamilton.

✻ It was called a 'circus' because the streets were first planned to be laid out in a circle – like a circus ring.

✻ Eros perches on top of the fountain (built 1893), holding a bow – but the sculptor gave him no arrows.

·❧ St Paul's Cathedral ❧·

DID YOU KNOW?

❋ The great west door to the cathedral is nine metres in height.

❋ At the top of the two western towers is a pineapple!

❋ The cathedral is built in the shape of a cross, and the central dome is over 100 metres high.

❋ Amongst those buried at St Paul's are Wellington, Nelson and Christopher Wren.

❋ When Wellington was buried there in 1852, one million people watched his funeral procession.

·❧ Albertopolis ❧·

From the profits of the Great Exhibition, Prince Albert – President of the Royal Commission – was responsible for the purchase of a chunk of land in the West of London on which a number of great museums were then built.

DID YOU KNOW?

  The area was nicknamed 'Albertopolis'.

The name of the main road, Exhibition Road, refers back to the Great Exhibition.

 The first director of the Victoria and Albert Museum was Henry Cole, whose little dog came to work with him at all times – and is buried in a garden in the centre of the museum.

 The Natural History Museum soon followed. It was opened in 1881 and described as a 'true Temple of Nature' by *The Times*.

·❧ The Royal Albert Hall ❧·

Planned as a music hall by Prince Albert – a great lover of music – the hall was named after his death by Queen Victoria when she laid the foundation stone in May 1867. But not everybody was impressed . . .

'A monstrous cross between the Colosseum, Rome, and a Yorkshire pie'
– *Saturday Review*, on the opening of the hall in 1870

People in the rookeries mostly keep clear of churches (although old Sol is reg'l'r as anything at his synagogue). The only time any of my friends are tempted in is when there is more than a bit of Bible on offer – and what I means is some nosh. It's amazing how many Hallelujahs a lad can abide if there's a pie to go with it, though the Gospel-men are likely to hand out a tract or two and such, or try and give us the 'errors with dire warnings about the fires of Hell and so forth. The fires of a baked tatur go down a lot better! Nobby folk, well, God seems to have a lot to do with rich people, possibly because they have full stomachs already when they kneel to pray so God has a lot less to do in return. Mind you, some of the missionaries are okay-types, but you have to watch out because they're likely to get you into a nice job, but I stand in awe in front of Miss Angela Burdett-Coutts, who has more money than creosote and spends all her time getting people into trades they can work in for a living and suchlike. It were her who taught me to read. She built little reading rooms so poor people could learn to read and write proper, and as you know, if you can read and write the world is your oyster, and I've eaten enough of those in my time 'cos they're so cheap.

Dodger to Angela Burdett-Coutts: 'I heard that Jesus walked on water, so he might know a little bit about toshing, but I ain't seen him down there. Mind you, in the dark you don't see everybody . . .'

Heaven above the clouds?

Afeard that there'd be very few costers among the angels, especially those lads whose silky words and sly hands (or the other way round?) had brought down a good girl, a coster girl explained her beliefs to Dodger's friend, Mister Henry Mayhew, by saying: 'When a good person is dying, we says "The Lord has called upon him, and he must go," but I can't think what it means, unless it is that an angel comes and tells the party he's wanted in heaven. I know where heaven is; it's above the clouds, and they're placed there to prevent us seeing into it.'

The filthy air wouldn't have helped either. Any angel foolish enough to have ventured through the fogs and down into the rookeries would soon have found their wings soiled with soot, probably making it quite difficult to take off again . . .

————·⚜ The Church of St Never* ⚜·————

> Debtors and bankers and politicians pray at the shrine
> of St Never.

Dodger did on occasion drop into the tiny church of St Never, in the little borough of Four Farthings (which was probably about the amount of money in the church's offertory box). The saint was supposedly in charge of things that never happened, and a number of naughty ladies would certainly go in and proffer a coin or two to St Never from time to time, but Mrs Holland was generally more reliable (though usually more expensive, her fees not always being in coinage).

————·⚜ Meeting One's Maker ⚜·————

Dodger knew of many people who had simply fallen down dead in the street, drowned in the river (like the unfortunate girls who leaped from bridges) or, like his old mentor, the tosher Grandad, donated themselves to the ratty congregation within the sewers. But London's graveyards were even more crowded than the flophouse, and noxious fumes were liable to rise from the overcrowded churchyards.

> The smell of death was a smell with a strange life of its own, and
> it would find its way in anywhere and it was damn hard to get
> rid of – rather, in some respects, like the smell of Onan . . .

*This church is a fictional place created by Terry Pratchett, as is the small borough of Four Farthings. Neither are real – but it would be nice to think that they did exist!

Winchester Geese

Crossbones Cemetery in Southwark was filled with the corpses of single women who hadn't just fallen as far down as the gutter but as deep as the grave. It was owned by the Bishop of Winchester and the poor girls were known as 'Winchester Geese'.

DID YOU KNOW?

 Corpses were often dug up within a week of being buried, chopped up and burned.

 Other bodies were sold to the hospitals and ended up under the scalpels of medical students.

 Up until 1823, suicides were often buried in the road with a stake banged through them, to stop the soul from wandering.

 'See you in Lavender' was a saying referring to Lavender Hill graveyard – and was often used as a threat (or a promise).

 Dentures were made from the teeth of the recently deceased, and one cove in Yorkshire (Edwin Clayton) managed to give his new teeth a second trip to the undertaker (and a third owner) when he died after swallowing the dentures.

Let them be buried ten deep, let us have a mausoleum!

Even in death, social class mattered in Dodger's London. To the nobby folk of London, a funeral was a serious business indeed – and with Queen Victoria pretty much in permanent mourning after Albert died, mourning also became a rather lengthy business. In 1832, seven private cemeteries – the 'Magnificent Seven' – were established in a ring around London, the nearest to Dodger being in Tower Hamlets. Now families could keep up with the neighbours (even the dead ones) by building elaborate memorials and family vaults.

- Families could hire an undertaker's mute; for a few pennies they would follow the coffin looking suitably sad. For a few more pennies they might even speak. For a shilling or more they would probably be prepared to sing like doves to see the soul on its way to Heaven.

- Terrified that they might be buried alive (it did happen!), those who could afford it arranged for a bell to be attached to the coffin so that they could ring for help if they woke up interred! Imagine walking through a graveyard and hearing the ring of a bell over a newly-dug grave . . .

Memento mori

In life, death is all around us – and memento mori were items to remind families of this (though in the rookeries, you didn't need to look far to see some evidence of mortality, a peek in the river often being sufficient). A lock of hair might be kept, or a favourite trinket, but as photography began to make its mark, the dead family member might have their photo taken several days after his or her death, sometimes even posed with other family members! No chance of ensuring the photographer caught their 'good side', then. With babies, the family might even keep the body until it mummified and then put it on display like an ornament – a family valuable any snakesman would decidedly leave untouched . . .

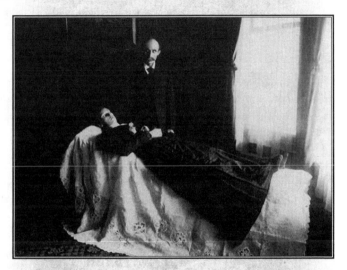

Superstitious?

Where death was concerned, the Victorians took not just the biscuit but the whole tin. Here are just a few:

- If a sparrow flies in and lands on a piano, someone in the house will die soon after.
- When someone dies, stop any clock in that room and cover the mirrors.
- When a funeral procession comes down the road, avoid meeting it head-on; if you can't turn round, you should hold a button until it has passed by.
- Thunder after a burial is a good sign – it means that the dearly departed's soul has reached heaven (at which point, presumably, it would be OK to dig them up again so as to have a bit more space).

I draw towards the close of my little guide with a quick glance at what might be up and coming for this magnificent city – a city I am proud to be a citizen of, and one which is moving forward so fast it's a miracle a body can keep his boots on the ground. In fact, as Miss Simplicity likes to point out to me, with railway trains steaming across the land, nobody actually needs to have their boots on the ground any more if choosing to travel, and that in itself is a wonder. I means, you can now get to High Wycombe in only one day! 'Cos in the olden days you'd have to go by coach and you'd be bound to find highwaymen around Loudwater. You don't get highwaymen on the railway.

'Changing times, Mister Dodger. A young queen on the throne and a new world of possibilities. Your world, should you choose to make it so' – *Angela Burdett-Coutts to Dodger*

·❧ Full Steam Ahead ❧·

A marvel of the Victorian age was the introduction of the railways. The first passenger trains had begun in the North of England in 1825, and by the end of the century almost every town in Britain had a railway station. Dodger set off to the West Country with Miss Simplicity on a coach pulled by horses, but by 1841 there was a railway line from London to Bristol. Not everyone believed they were safe, though . . .

THE GREAT TICKET DELAY

'A long, close-packed, and agitated *queue* of passengers is in waiting [. . .] a traveller arriving in good time, must watchfully linger in a dreary and draughty corridor until it pleases the haughty young gentleman within the rabbit-hutch to raise the hatch thereof. A traveller arriving rather late, must take his place at the end of a long "tail" of eager and angry applicants, with much probability of getting his ticket just in time to lose the train.'

– PUNCH (1882)

RAILWAY UNDERTAKING.

Touter. "Going by this Train, Sir?"   *Passenger.* "'M? Eh? Yes."
Touter. "Allow me, then, to give you one of my Cards, Sir."

·❧ Going Underground ❧·

Dodger's world beneath the streets saw some huge changes as the underground train lines began to be built. 1863 saw the opening of the first underground trains of the Metropolitan Railway and a huge number of Londoners queued up to get tickets.

* Every station along the line was crowded with hopeful passengers. By noon there were enough people waiting at Paddington to fill four trains, and by the end of the day nearly 25,000 people had enjoyed the new experience!
* Gas lights were installed in the carriages so that passengers would feel less alarmed at the journey through the tunnels – especially the ladies, who feared that young gentlemen could Take Advantage.
* Passengers had been told that there would be no steam or smoke coming into the carriages, but on these first journeys those on board were subject to clouds of steam – most unpleasant.

·❧ Marvels for Everyone ❧·

As the century progressed, it was *amazing* what people could think up – labour-saving devices that made life a whole lot easier, and a few that didn't quite make the grade . . .

A cold bath in the morning?

Imagine being woken by ringing bells, then tipped by your automated mattress into a bath of cold water! That was the design of cabinet-maker Theophilus Carter's alarm-clock bed, first shown at the Great Exhibition in 1851. Everyone at the Exhibition was much cheered by watching the demonstrations (everybody except the poor nobody who was paid to be flung into the water at regular intervals, that is).

DID YOU KNOW?

Carter was known to stand in the door of his furniture shop wearing a top hat, and it is believed that Lewis Carroll based the character of the Mad Hatter in *Through the Looking-Glass* on him. For ever after, everyone in Oxford – where his shop was – called him the 'Mad Hatter'.

Two for the price of one?

Not much space in your crib? Perhaps you would find a combination cot and step-ladder useful?

·——— COMBINATION COT AND STEP-LADDER. ———·

We have had lots of clever inventions for saving room in small houses, but the most original is certainly this combination of a bed and a step-ladder. It should prove a very useful article where the occupant of the bed is a light sleeper and doesn't mind having to get up when the step-ladder is needed. It might also be useful in very large families where chairs were scarce . . . With the addition of a strong wire spring attached to an alarm clock, it should also make an excellent servants' bed. At 6:30 every morning the alarm would work the spring, and the bed immediately be transformed into a pair of steps. This would promote habits of punctuality and early rising in domestic servants that would be invaluable to them.

– **Extract from** *The Great Round World and What Is Going on in It* **magazine** (1897), 'Invention and Discovery' section

Prefer a bang on the head instead?

An 1882 device took a different – but equally painful – approach. A clock was attached to a frame over the head of the person in bed, and at the appropriate moment, down came the frame! The blow was supposed to be light enough to wake anyone up, though not to hurt . . .

The hostess with . . . the smokiest rooms!

Since smoking was so popular – the Victorians thought it was a healthy habit and had no idea how many early deaths it would bring about – any hostess worth a fig needed to fill her rooms with clouds of smoke from varied types of tobacco. But if no one in the household smoked, well, a machine was available which could smoke cigars for you . . .

Multi-tasking for a gentleman

If a gentleman should choose to leave the smoky fug of the drawing room and go for a walk instead, now there was a handy gadget available.

With this, any well-to-do gentleman could go for a walk *and* play the flute, measure a horse or capture a butterfly, *even if it was raining.*

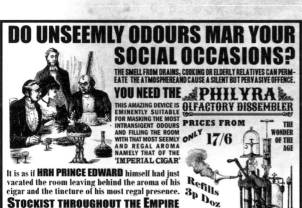

*In which I conclude by introducing you to just a few of the most forward-thinkers of my time,
some of whom I was lucky enough to meet at Miss Angela's home in Mayfair.*

Sir George Cayley (1773–1857)

Often called the man who discovered flight, Cayley looked at how birds flew and decided there was no reason why people shouldn't do the same. To this end he built a working glider, then a small biplane (which apparently a ten-year-old boy piloted), before moving on to a bigger glider.

Charles Babbage (1791–1871)

'A rather taciturn gentleman who looks as if he lost a guinea and found a farthing' – *Angela Burdett-Coutts*

Dodger could reckon his numbers as much as a body needed to if living in the rookeries – often biting into coins to see if they were really silver was better than trying to add them up – but Mister Babbage began to make machines that would mean that no one needed to have to add up by themselves again.

His first calculating engine – which he never actually finished – was called a 'difference engine' and weighed about 15 tons, being around 8 feet in height. So, not exactly a calculator you could put in a pocket . . .

DID YOU KNOW?

While at Cambridge University, Babbage joined several clubs, including the Ghost Club – ghost-hunting! – and the Extractors Club, which made sure that any member would be freed if they were committed to an insane asylum (possibly after a spot of ghost-hunting?).

Ada Lovelace (1815–52)

Ada was the daughter of Lord Byron. Her mother – who had studied mathematics – decided that her daughter should also learn about the sciences. Ada grew up to work with Babbage on his analytical engines and to show the world that women could be great mathematicians too.

DID YOU KNOW?

- She signed her work as A. A. L. so that no one would know she was a woman.
- Many years later, the United States named a computer language 'Ada' in her honour.

Isambard Kingdom Brunel (1806–59)

An inventor and engineer who changed the face of Britain for many. But few knew he was also a dab hand at conjuring tricks – though on one occasion he accidentally swallowed a half-sovereign while doing tricks for his children. He rapidly assembled a board between two uprights, strapped himself to it and spun round and round until the centrifugal force made the coin shoot back out.

And as Sol explained it me, with the right investment from people like Miss Angela, the ideas of men and women like this could take flight and their ideas would help bring London kicking and shouting into a new world of invention and creation, and opportunities, even for a lad like myself with an 'umble birth. For where there is an idea, there tends to be a bit of a gamble, and where there's a gamble, there must surely always be room for sharp and clever Dodgers . . .

London isn't all that big when you think about it: a square mile of mazes, surrounded by even more streets and people and . . . opportunities.

If you liked my notes, you might like to take a gander at some of these books by other scribblers, including my old pals Mister Charlie and Mister Mayhew . . .

Thomas Beames, *The Rookeries of London* (1852)

Alfred Rosling Bennett, *London and Londoners in the Eighteen-Fifties and Sixties* (1920)*

Peter Cunningham, *Hand-Book of London* (1850)

Charles Dickens, *David Copperfield* (1850)

Charles Dickens, *Great Expectations* (1861)

Charles Dickens, *The Letters of Charles Dickens*, vol. V (1847–9)

Charles Dickens, *Sketches from Boz* (1836)

Charles Dickens Jnr, *Dickens's Dictionary of London* (1879)

W. S. Gilbert, *London Characters and the Humorous Side of Life* (c.1870)

James Greenwood, *Mysteries of London* (1883)

James Greenwood, *The Seven Curses of London* (1869)

James Greenwood, *Toilers in London* (1883)

Daniel Joseph Kirwan, *Palace and Hovel: Phases of London Life* (1878)

A. Lady, *Beauty: What It Is, and How to Retain It* (1873)

Henry Mayhew, *London Labour and the London Poor* (1851–61)

George R. Sims, *Living London* (1901)

Thomas Webster, *An Encyclopaedia of Domestic Economy* (1845)

Andrew Wynter, *Pictures of Town & Country Life, and other papers* (1865)

And some of these other publications . . .

The *Era*

The *Morning Post*

Punch magazine

The *Tomahawk*

The *Saturday Review*

The Great Round World and What Is Going on in It

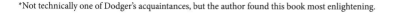

*Not technically one of Dodger's acquaintances, but the author found this book most enlightening.

LIST OF ILLUSTRATIONS, BY PAGE

THE AUTHOR ALSO MADE OCCASIONAL USE OF THESE MORE MODERN NOTES . . .

www.victorianweb.org
www.victorianlondon.org
www.history.co.uk/explore-history/ history-of-london
www.eastlondonhistory.com
http://blogs.smithsonianmag.com/ history
http://eudocs.lib.byu.edu
http://journals.cambridge.org
http://londonbygaslight.wordpress. com/2011
http://louderthanwar.com/20-weird-facts-about-parliament
http://myweb.tiscali.co.uk/speel/london
http://vcp.e2bn.org/justice
www.howitworksdaily.com/history

www.aboutbritain.com/articles
www.avictorian.com
www.arthurlloyd.co.uk
www.cityoflondon.gov.uk
www.pedalinghistory.com
www.bbc.co.uk/history
www.bethlemheritage.org.uk
www.bog-standard.org
www.british-history.ac.uk
www.jubileecampaign.co.uk
www.listverse.com
www.londononline.co.uk/streetorigins
www.met.police.uk/history
www.oldbaileyonline.org
www.open.ac.uk/Arts/history-from-police-archives

www.portcities.org.uk/london
www.puppetonline.co.uk/ punchandjudyhistory.html
www.rhymes.org.uk
www.royal.gov.uk
www.sewerhistory.org
www.stpauls.com
www.timeout.com
www.tlucretius.net/Sophie/Castle/ victorian_slang.html
www.victorianblogspot.co.uk
www.workhouses.org.uk